JAZZ A·B·Z

WYNTON MARSALIS
and
PAUL ROGERS

with biographical sketches by
Phil Schaap

PUBLISHED BY CANDLEWICK PRESS, CAMBRIDGE MASSACHUSETTS

To Wynton, Simeon, and Jasper — W. M.
To Alex and Nate — P. R.

Text copyright © 2005 by Wynton Marsalis

Biographical sketches text copyright © 2005 by Phil Schaap

Illustrations copyright © 2005 by Paul Rogers

Book design by Jill von Hartmann

First edition 2005

Library of Congress Cataloging-in-Publication Data

Marsalis, Wynton, date.

Jazz A-B-Z: an A to Z collection of jazz portraits / Wynton Marsalis; illustrated by Paul Rogers; with biographical sketches by Phil Schaap. — 1st ed.

p.   cm.

ISBN 0-7636-2135-8

1. Jazz musicians — Juvenile poetry. 2. Children's poetry, American. 3. Jazz — Juvenile poetry. I. Rogers, Paul. II. Schaap, Phil. III. Title.

PS3613.A7696J39 2005

811'.6 – dc22   2005048448

4 6 8 10 9 7 5 3

Printed in China

This book was typeset in Myriad.

The illustrations were done in acrylic and ink.

Candlewick Press

2067 Massachusetts Avenue

Cambridge, Massachusetts 02140

visit us at www.candlewick.com

A NOTE FROM PAUL ROGERS

I'm sitting in a dark theater watching a ballet production of *Swan Lake* with my wife, Jill. It's beautiful, but it isn't really my scene, so my mind wanders. I start thinking about the music that I really love—jazz music. Can I think of a jazz musician for every letter of the alphabet without leaving any of the *giant* giants off the list? *A* is for *Armstrong*—a good start. *B* is for *Basie*. . . . I begin to make my way through the alphabet, matching letters to first or last names and nicknames. While I'm doing this in my head, I begin to see images of the musicians mixed up with letter forms.

The next day I write the list down and start thinking that it would make an interesting book. My idea is to design a portrait of each musician in a style that gives a sense of his or her sound and also reflects a particular period in time. I also decide it can't be just a book of images—I want to use words to create a dialogue with the paintings. I know immediately that there would be no one better suited for this collaboration than Wynton Marsalis. I have learned so much about jazz from listening to Wynton's music and to the musicians he admires. We met on a project a few years before and always managed to stay in touch. So I call him up and describe the idea for the book. It takes him about one minute to agree to write something to accompany the paintings.

Over the next few years, I work on the book between assignments. Whenever Wynton and I see each other, I remind him that he has some writing to do. When the paintings are finally done, I send copies to Wynton. I start getting these meticulously handwritten poems faxed from various locations around the world—he's been writing after gigs and while he's on the road. I don't know what I was expecting, but these are way beyond my imagination. You'll see.

From the very beginning, the hardest part was not leaving anyone off the list. Some, I knew had to be a part of it—Duke, Miles, Monk, Billie. But for every artist on the list, there are so many who should also be included. And even now, I'm still thinking of all the musicians I love who are not in the book: Benny Carter, Art Tatum, Max Roach, Bud Powell, Ben Webster, Ray Charles, Hank Jones, Nina Simone, Dexter Gordon, Abbey Lincoln, Gil Evans, Clifford Brown, Jon Hendricks, Mary Lou Williams, Bill Evans . . .

Paul Rogers

I met Paul Rogers in 1990. We hit it off right away and began a friendship fueled by a mutual love of jazz and art. Down through these fifteen years, we frequently talked about collaborating on some type of music-painting book. Knowing that talk often leads to just more talk, Paul decided to paint an alphabet book of portraits featuring some of the most colorful and provocative personalities in jazz. I received the completed book with a note: "What are you going to do about this, and when?" After too much time had passed, I considered writing some songs in the style of each musician. But then I figured, why do that when their material speaks so definitively for *all* of who they were?

I got deeper into Paul's paintings for direction. They are rich in symbolism, filled with references to song titles, artifacts, and hallowed places that powerfully evoke the originality of the musicians' spirits and the spirit of their times—the gardenia that Billie Holliday elegantly wore in her hair; Sonny Rollins at the Williamsburg Bridge, where he practiced during a three-year retirement. Paul's Sarah Vaughan recalls those concert advertisement posters that would illegally show up on every telephone pole or bus stop in the community when I was a boy. He even plays with different styles of portraits that connect jazz musicians to great artists who loved jazz—Stuart Davis, for example, whose syncopated style is implied in the portrait of Charles Mingus. The diversity of styles and the richness of jazz mythology in each portrait inspired me to write some poems, and to give every letter a different poetic form related in some way to the musician's style of playing or being. Basie loved the blues, so his poem is a blues poem. Coltrane liked to reel off long lines related to a basic theme, so his poem is a list poem. Jelly Roll loved to brag about himself, so his poem is an ode. You see what I mean?

I love playing with musical ideas, and I love playing with words. Writing these poems was so much fun! I love to read the poetry of W. B. Yeats out loud. Most of the time I read his poems to entertain the great photographer Frank Stewart and our road manager, an American classic, Raymond "Big Boss" Murphy, as we drive all over the United States. I'm talking about twenty- and thirty-hour drives from Seattle to Philadelphia. I keep them awake at three or four in the morning through hail, sleet, and snow, playing and clowning around. I'd like to thank them for listening to these poems and helping me shape them up so Paul would like them. I asked Frank and "Big Boss," "Is this phrase better than the one I had before?" And, whatever they would say, I'd ask them again. Then they would say, "It was cool, man. It was cool before, too. Shut up and go to sleep." But about 4:43 in the morning, they'd wake me up and say, "Hey, man. Read us *H* again."

Armstrong.

Armstrong almighty!

An ad-libbing acrobat.

American ambassador of affirmation.

Adventurous author of ambrosial aires.

Absolute architect of the Jazz Age.

Almighty Armstrong attacks a trumpet with abandon!

Armstrong's amazing artistry astonishes audiences of all ages.

Africa to Asia, Australia to Argentina, and even Armenia,

Ambassador Armstrong animates the altitudes with angular aural arabesques aplenty.

Awkward adagio arias adjusted with agile allegro accents appease Armstrong's admirers.

Anybody asks, tell them Armstrong almighty is aglow amidst the angels above.

Bouncin' with my baby to Basie's Big Time Band,

Bouncin' with my baby to Basie's Big Time Band,

Rhythm is their business, but the blues is their brand.

Up from Kansas City with a buttoned-down four-four swing,

Up from Kansas City with a buttoned-down four-four swing,

Brilliant brass blazin' and that boom-boom! bass drum thing.

Baked beans and barbecue and a big brown bass below,

Baked beans and barbecue and a big brown bass below,

Best be back behind the beat when Basie's band begins to blow.

Prez, both Franks and Papa Jo are standing in the wings.

Prez, both Franks and Papa Jo are standing in the wings.

'Bout to brew the beastly groove that Basie always brings.

Sweets and Buck and Snooky Young and a bone man named Al Grey,

Sweets and Buck and Snooky Young and a bone man named Al Grey,

Burnished bells boast and blare that Basie's come to play.

Hey Count Basie! Basie what you got to say?

Hey Count Basie! Basie what you got to say?

Bouncin' with my baby, 'bout to swing the blues away.

Coltrane is a country boy come calling on the big city.

      Aww but couldn't he croon a campground tune with ironclad candor?

      But couldn't he caress a popular melody with cold-blooded compassion?

      Couldn't he conjure up the ceremonial clamor of churchy Carolina congregations!

Coltrane is a country boy quite chilly in the cold coast city.

      Aww but couldn't he construct a comprehensive course of study to conquer the
            incompliant techniques of the tenor saxophone?

      But couldn't he call upon a colossal capacity to concentrate?

      Couldn't he practice and practice and incessantly practice his craft
            with uncompromising conviction?

Coltrane, country as cornbread, collard greens, fried chicken, cane, and even
            chitlins, is celebrated in the big city as upcoming
            champion of scales, clefs, and cutting-edge concepts.

      Aww but couldn't he capsize calcified conventions and challenge the contrarian campus critics?

      But couldn't he create controversy amongst the condescending cognoscenti,
            the (chatty) clever, the certified, and the (merely) competent?

      Couldn't he just keep on cascading through closely clustered chord
            changes, cartwheeling through complex, careening, chromatic calculations?

Coltrane is a comet, a constellation, a cherished citizen of the cosmos.

      Aww but couldn't he cackle and cry and scream freedom up the chock-full core
            of a volcanic cadenza?

      But couldn't he hot-comb the creases out of a cheeky classic and
            completely captivate a packed-to-capacity corner club?

      Couldn't he coax and cajole common sense out of a corrupted
            culture and crusade for our country's long-in-the-coming civil rights?

Coltrane was a country boy come to the big city 'come lost in the stars.

      Aww but couldn't he cram a century of conflict and confusion into a
            compelling catechism to convert charlatans?

      But couldn't he corkscrew cacophonous currents of clearly
            channeled consciousness through a cookie-cutter
            community of too-cerebral concertgoers
            seeking change or a cheap charge?

      Couldn't he cook up a cauldron of convoluted callaloo to
            confound the casual fan and curious recruit
            alike with cosmic cubist counterpoint,
            incomprehensible crescendoing of cymbals,
            ceaseless chaos, crisscrossed columns of
            sonic calculus, and a stormy sea of collective
            concerns come crashing down to chase the crazy crowd away!

Maybe dance
music draws
major dimes.
Merry disco
might drive
moody dupes
manic. Ditzy!
Motto: *Dough*
makes dopes
money drunk.
Muted drama
mixes Delta
moans, demon
myths, dummy
media, drums,
magic, Dixie
mumbo, droll
Monks, Dizzy,
me-too. Dogma
molds dense
minds, doles
moral decay.
Modal daddy
mints dreck.
Mercy! Didn't
Midas dream
madly? Ditto
Miles Davis.

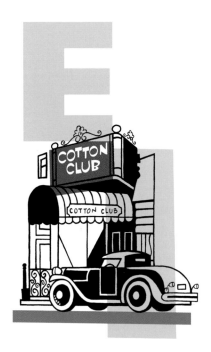

Ellington is a most elegant man

Suit, shirt, and shoes, slicked-back hair spic-and-span

Perfect pressed trousers and tie tied just right

Even his casual clothes outta sight.

With an eloquent pen Duke expresses his views

Compositions extending the ethos of blues

From *Concerto for Cootie* to *Black, Brown and Beige*

Be it eighth notes or whole notes embossing the page.

Duke's cats — C.T., Ray Nance, each one

Big Ben, round Rex, who else? Blanton

Northeast, wild west, sweet south the same

"Come swing," he called; New York they came.

The Orchestra evokes New Orleans nights

Exotica of Egypt, Paris sights

Esteemed ensemble, everyone elite

Exuding pure emotion bittersweet.

Eager to exclaim the joy of jazz they swing with ease embarking

on a string of one-night gigs nonstop for years at the expense of every

everything: to educate, to elevate, to urge the earthbound ear

and heart alike to soar, to etch the evidence of

the eternal Ellington effect upon the ether and the core

and to erect, encrypt, enshrine an aural monument forevermore.

DUKE Ellington

What of?

> *Of the fortuitous, of the fragility of a moment . . .*

PREACHER: And did we find ourselves flung
> face to face with some finely tuned female voice,
> formless and forever, defying Father Time and all known laws of physics,
> floaty and fabulous, phrasing with feather-edged finesse some fantastic fable
> fetched from the pre-primeval forests of fairyhood?

CONGREGATION: *Yes, yes we did.*

PREACHER: She before us. Fine, infinite, and fluorescent—in fact, incandescent.
> Flesh and blood become ephemeral through the
> unfathomable beauty of a sound.
> Fluffy, flavorful, and fluent. And firm and fertile.
> Furthermore, full, fiery, flammable like the feet of a
> flamenquero at final flourish.

And did that voice take flight, friends?

CONGREGATION: *Yessuh, oh yes. It did.*

PREACHER: And then the false façade of formality or an even faker forced
> *in*formality begins to falter and finally to fold.
> Faced with that ferocious, fantastic, flying force,
> our souls flutter off afree.

And then, the feeling of fainting or falling
> infinitely through some forbidden
> or long-forgotten memory before it fades.

And did we follow that feeling further and
> further into a flickering confounded fractured fuzziness?

CONGREGATION: *Have mercy, yes. Oh yes Lord, yes!*

PREACHER: And did we forestall the fleet-footed folly of
> floating off to far-fetched, far-out corners of our own consciousness,
> never to be found,
> trapped by some femme fatale with a transfixing song?
> Frozen in time?

CONGREGATION: *Confess it.*

PREACHER: Tell her. Tell her but do not flatter.
> No flirty fleet-footed flim-flammery.
> > No flippant flimsy counterfeit shim-shammery.
> > > Tell her how **fearless** she makes you feel.

And did we find ourselves back in a flash,
> beyond the footlights,
> > fiending for the next song?

ALL TOGETHER: *Ahhh yes . . . The Great Fitzgerald.*

There was a grand gentleman Gerry

a great saxophone dignitary

whose glorious tone

did the gaffers bemoan

while the guys and the gals all made merry.

A giant of saxophone baritone

of grinding a groove to the grisly bone

'cross the globe did he gig —

a jazz gypsy you dig?—

this genius whose gifts were full blown.

He blew with a cool gentle attitude

blue nuggets whose glimmering pulchritude

gave the gals goo-goo eyes

tit-for-tat got the guys

and a gaggle of gossip ensued . . .

By the grace of a Mulligan mood.

Coleman Hawkins came to New York from Missouri. He joined Fletcher Henderson's Orchestra. He became known as the "Father of the Jazz Saxophone." Mr. Hawkins was a virtuoso capable of first-class improvisations on all types of music. He was a stylish dresser. Musicians called him "Bean," meaning he was very intelligent.

■ ■ ■

The Hawk, a high-born hellion sportin' a handcrafted headpiece is

hightailin' it to the Big Apple from some hick-haven in the heartland.

Most hometown heroes hasten to the Big Town to have their say, to handle up,

to do handiwork Jack, wreak havoc. Man, those high-flying

hopefuls receive a hearty helping of the Big City beatdown.

A hickory hardwood heads-up: "Hey! Homepiece, hold up!

You came up here all huffy and handsome, hoping to be heralded; now you're

haggard, hurt, and humbled. Hard-pressed and homesick." Here, however,

is the Hawk. He's no hillbilly hack hankering to hopelessly hustle in

some Harlem hellhole. Oh no! Lookee here Jim. Hawk's not even in New York a *half*-minute

till he's hired by Fletcher Henderson hisself!! Well, Henderson's men,

haughty, high-falutin', high-rollerin' hipsters, have no eyes for any hyped-up

hoop-ti-doo home-corn hotshots. So Hawk, headstrong, high-strung, and holy,

breaks hog-wild on his first solo. He high-steps through a hot hailstorm of heavy

head-slapping harmonic hurdles. "Huh?" (That's them.) Then with his hypnotic, husky,

hot-blooded tone, the honey-tongued Hawk heats up a sweet slow one that could

heal all heartaches and humanize the happy heathen. "Hah!" (That's Hawk.)

Henderson's men are hooked. They called Hawk "Bean." That's right. The headmaster,

the head honcho. Hawk did headwork, man. He's a heavyweight. Honest.

brrrrrrrrrrrrrrrrrrrrrrrrrrrrrrrrr **BANG BOOM !**

Snare drum press roll.

Impassioned invention of mine own imagination.

Initiator of emotion,

irrupting from silence to an instant inferno of ecstasy.

With this innovative imprint of my incontestable individuality,

"I empower improvisations. I illuminate time.

I inspire the initiates and inform the inexperienced.

I invoke the intuitive intelligence of the immortals."

	x		x		x		x
ting	tinky	ting	tinky	ting	tinky	ting	tinky
	x		x		x		x
ting	ch	ting	ch-ky	ting	ch	ting	ch-ky
	x		x		x		x
Boom!	ch	Boom!	ch	Boom!	ch		ch
	x		x		x		x
	ch		ch	Boom!	Boom!	Boom!	Boom!
	x		x		x		x
			ch		ch	Bam!	ch	ch

I am Abdullah Ibn Buhaina. They call me Art Blakey.

Icon imperial of the divine instrument of independence.

I am.

	1	2	3	4	1	2	3	4
(snap fingers)		x		x		x		x
(count silently)	1	2	3	4	1	2	3	4
(keep snapping)		x		x		x		x
	ting	tinky	ting	tinky	ting	tinky	ting	tinky
		x		x		x		x
	ting	ch	ting	ch-ky	ting	ch	ting	ch-ky
		x		x		x		x
	Boom!	ch	Boom!	ch	Boom!	ch		ch
		x		x		x		x
		ch		ch		ch		ch
		x		x		x		x
	Boom!	Boom!	Boom!	Boom!	Boom!	ch	ch	
		x		x				
		ch		ch				

(turn page)

I am Abdullah Ibn Buhaina, icon imperial of drums
and the indestructible, ineluctable, fine art of swing.

	x		x		x		x	x			x
ting	tinky	ting	tinky	ting	tinky	ting	tinky	tinky	ting	ting	ting

I inflame icy metal cymbals with an insistent beat dividing time into swingtime,

	x		x
tinky	ting	tinky	ting

each intense iteration an indelible imprint of my integrity.

	x		x		x		x		x		x
mm	ch	mm	ch	mm	ch	mm	ch	mm	ch	mm	ch

Internal clock called sock cymbal
invigorates the swing with an infallible pulse.
It locks the time in tight.

	x		x		x		x		x		x		x
Boom		Boom		Boom				Boom	Boom	Boom	Boom	Boom	

Uh-oh! Thunder — incoming. The Big Boom!
My bass drum can blacken a big man's eye and injure
a hero's pride. The inductor, it infiltrates time,
impugns the impassive, and irradiates the uninspired.

	x		x		x		x	x	x	x	x		x	
Bang!		Bang!		Bang!		Bang!						Bang!		Bang!

The ionizer. My crash cymbal is lightning itself.
Interruptor of the by and by with one incendiary idea:
"I electrify time." Invite the Big Boom, and thunder and lightning
will ignite the bandstand with uncontrollable intensity.

		x		x		x		x
(snap fingers)								
(count silently)	1	2	3	4	1	2	3	4
(keep snapping)		x		x		x		x
	ting	tinky	ting	tinky	ting	tinky	ting	tinky
		x		x		x		x
	ting	ch	ting	ch-ky	ting	ch	ting	ch-ky
		x		x		x		x
	Boom!	ch	Boom!	ch	Boom!	ch		ch
		x		x		x		x
		ch		ch		ch		ch
		x		x		x		x
	Boom!	Boom!	Boom!	Boom!	Boom!	ch	ch	
		x		x				
		ch		ch				

(turn page)

I am Abdullah Ibn Buhaina, icon imperial of drums
    and the indestructible, ineluctable, fine art of swing.

```
           x          x          x          x          x          x          x
   ting  tinky  ting  tinky  ting  tinky  ting  tinky  tinky  ting  ting  ting
```

I inflame icy metal cymbals with an insistent beat dividing time into swingtime,

```
          x          x
   tinky  ting  tinky  ting
```

each intense iteration an indelible imprint of my integrity.

```
        x        x        x        x        x        x
   mm   ch   mm  ch   mm  ch   mm  ch   mm  ch   mm  ch
```

Internal clock called sock cymbal
invigorates the swing with an infallible pulse.
It locks the time in tight.

```
         x          x          x          x        x     x     x       x       x
   Boom       Boom       Boom            Boom  Boom  Boom  Boom  Boom
```

Uh-oh! Thunder — incoming. The Big Boom!
My bass drum can blacken a big man's eye and injure
a hero's pride. The inductor, it infiltrates time,
impugns the impassive, and irradiates the uninspired.

```
         x          x          x          x     x     x     x     x       x        x
   Bang!      Bang!      Bang!      Bang!                         Bang!    Bang!
```

The ionizer. My crash cymbal is lightning itself.
Interruptor of the by and by with one incendiary idea:
"I electrify time." Invite the Big Boom, and thunder and lightning
will ignite the bandstand with uncontrollable intensity.

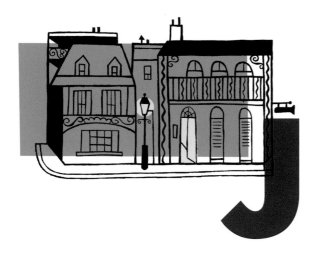

January evening

jet-black moonless night

jam-packed joint—

jukebox jangling junk.

Jane, Janice, and Jeretha jiggle through the joint

jotting down orders.

A joker named Junior tends bar;

Jerks jostle and jibe.

Juiceheads jiggle their lil' change to judge the possibilities of

just one more julep.

We joust with the crowd for our favorite corner table.

Jambalaya and jalapeño smother the air.

Northern businessmen on a junket crack juvenile jokes and a

jerry-built bandstand juts out onto a small dance floor.

Me, a journalist friend, and a couple of journeymen jitterbuggers

waiting for the jam session jaw about everything from Jamestown

to John Coltrane.

A juggler trying for tips vies with

a juju lady plying head trips.

Lights jimble when lightning bolts and a reverberant silence

jolts the room in a winking moment, then . . .

The talk turns to Jelly Roll. Jelly Roll and jazz.

Jumbo giant—creole dreamer who turned jargon into gospel.

Jester and genius in one and Jesuit and juggernaut, too!

Who could solve the jillion-pieced jigsaw puzzle called jazz with

a few dancing dots on paper, then justify a glittering jewel

in his front tooth?

Who journeyed from one end of this country to the other,

a one-man jamboree

pattin' juba, raggin' jigs, jumpin' rigs, and hustlin' gigs?

He ward off jinxes with High John,

ride jitney in a jam, him jive the jealous in a jiffy,

and jape the judge if him can.

Now the jitterbugs join hands and jitter on away.

Me and my journalist friend Jasper continue to say,

Who unjumbled the jigsaw puzzle of backroom jive

that turned the truth out and spilled out lies?

Who? with jazzy little notes on paper kept a journal of life

for the average Joe and stuck-up socialite—

Who jellified the boiling jungle of do-gooders and

no-good-for-nothings alike that

jeer at the just but adjourn as the jury?

Who lifted Jezebel's jaded heart with sultry Spanish song and

jazzed all the rags from New Orleans to Missouri,

syncopated a stiff, tight, corny march, and

jobbed a whole town with snake oil,

jerry juice, and a Crescent City sound?

Who juked and joshed playing the dozens by twos, even

jeopardize his own life stealing jazz from the blues?

Just *who* is a Janus-walkin' one-man jubilee?

Ain't nobody but Jelly set the slaves free.

King Oliver, reigning monarch of the Crescent City cornet,

>*in the back bar of a club on Kentucky Street*

>*holds court. A collegiate acolyte seeks an audience*

>*with the King. Here's the Big Kahuna giving a*

>*not-so-kindly-keynote:* You knuckle-headed, knock-kneed,

>careless, kindergarten klutz, kick back and let the kind Kaiser

>of cornet tell you this much. You have the ambitions of a knight

>but the talents of a kidney. The roar of a lion but the bite of a

>kitten. You were keeper of the flame when it became a smoking

>wick. The doctor who birthed you gave you a knee-deep kick.

>Kidnappers paid your momma's ransom note. She took the

>cash, then gave you your coat.

>>College, it kills me to speak this way. I hate to

>be a killjoy, but that's okay. The princess kissed a toad and

>you became a snake. The chick you considered to be your wife

>met the proposal with a calamitous moan, "Go fly a kite to

>parts unknown, then get lost and keep right on."

The Khalif of cornet continues to crack: If looks could kill, you'd be a

>walking plague. Son, you have the presence of a knot and the

>personality of kale. But before this shellacking gets too good to me, let the

>Kublai Khan of cornet resyncopate some comments on how you play.

>I traveled from the top of Kilimanjaro to the bottom of Kalamazoo,

>seeking any anyone half as sad as you. Kept on trying, if you only knew,

>then came across a crazy kleptomaniac with a store-bought kazoo.

>Even he was better, but not his kangaroo. One final word for you

>and your ilk (kumquat-headed kids in a club drinking chocolate milk).

>This is why I'm the King and you're all quarry:

>>I seek kingdoms and y'all seek kennels.

>>Keep your horn in the case, Knave!

Lazy, listless, languishing longly

laying low and all alone.

Losing at love and living. I'm

lost in life. . . . Lost and left alone.

Last-ditch lyrics idle on a low frequency, liminal song.

It's a Lady.

Lady Bountiful leading the lilting lullaby,

Lady of the Lake with letter-perfect delivery,

Ladies Luna and Sol, luminous as the day is long,

It's Lady Day.

She lavishes loving-kindness on a lonely lament.

Languid becomes luscious; lackluster, luxuriant.

Limp becomes lively; a little — a lot. And

laughter lifts longing

all because a relentless lady loosed liquid life

on lines of mulish melody and lugubrious language

to deliver me from lasting lovelessness.

Should I laud my lady with gold leaf clusters?

      With a lavaliere of lapis lazuli

      or lotus and lilac poems?

Well, let me applaud my Lady Day in song:

      Always will I love you and love to always love you.

Mingus makes mad, majestic, mind-boggling music.

Mystic mulatto music on matter-of-factly marked manuscript.

Measured manuscript in major and minor modes mostly made up in a
    mysterious moment by miracle men.

Magic men with musical instruments that moan and mock and moo.

Merry mooing or moaning mellow melancholic moods or even more
    miscellaneous mish-mashed emotions.

Mother Goose meets Mardi Gras and

Mingus makes mighty, maddening, muscular music.

Maelstroms of romantic music like when the blues marries
    meat-and-potatoes with multi-mathematic modulations.

Metric modulations mandating mind-bending rhythmic mastery.

Mental mastery of motifs melding multifarious moments.

Mercurial moments matching moralists and mercenaries, militants and minstrels,
    mercy and murder, mud and the moon.

Mesopotamia meets Manhattan and

Mingus makes musky, misbehaving, mesmerizing, maniacal music.

Moorish mythic music — Malayalam — mixing metaphysical modern modes and
    marketable mainstream melodies.

Mollycoddled milky melodies marinated in mischief and much
    much macumba.

Mexican macumba masquerading as mambo mown on a massive bull fiddle.

Magnificent fiddling of misanthrope and martyr and mouthy
    megalomaniac and most moral minister of mumbo jumbo.

Man of God meets Man o' War. Martin meets Malcolm and Mandela
    *meets . . . **Man!***

Mingus might just talk about your momma, then go 'head and
    manifest a masterpiece by midnight. . . . Maybe.

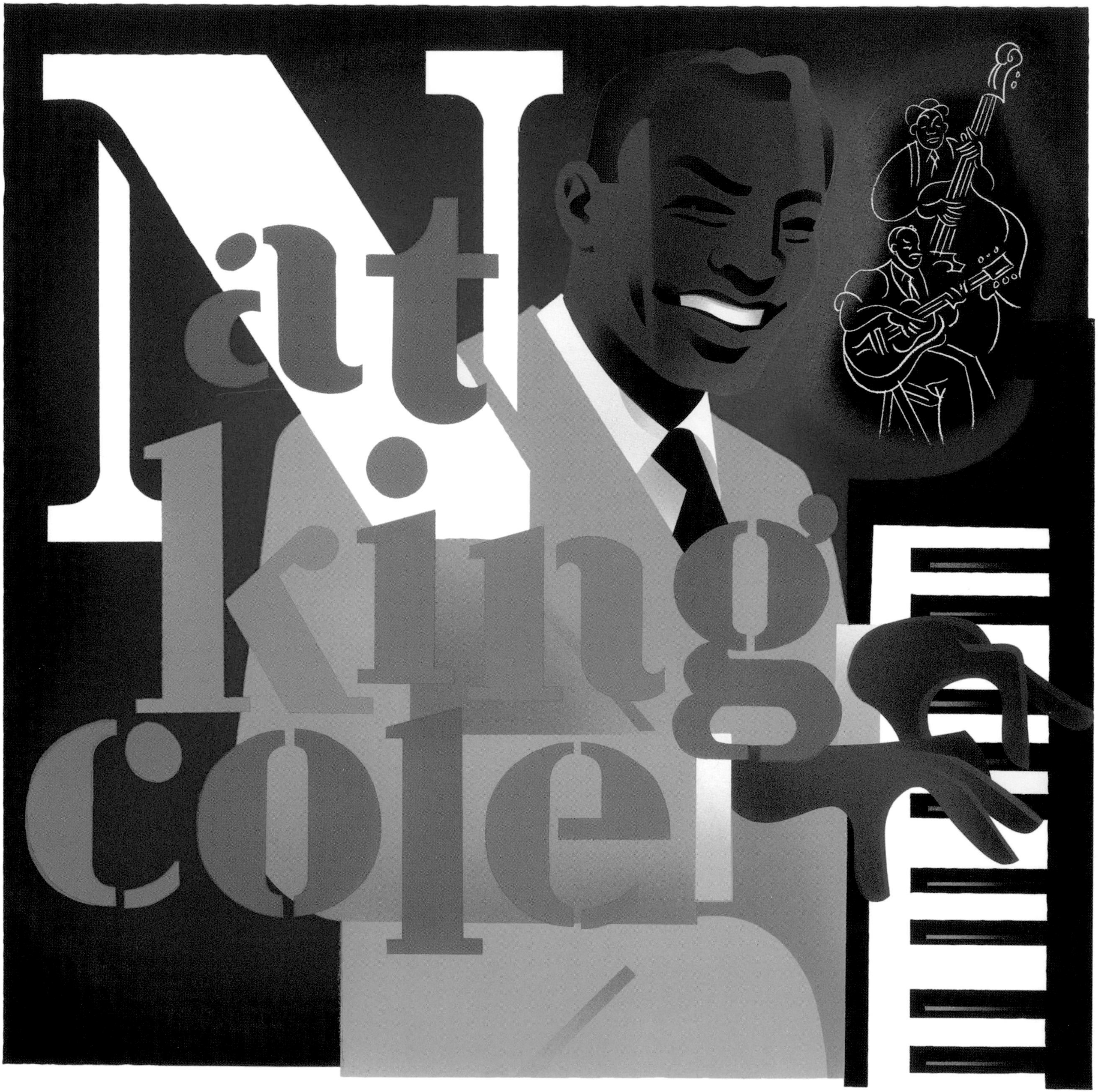
Nat
king
cole

Ol' King Cole set a notable goal

and a noteworthy goal set he.

Oh he yearned for a bass

and a string guitar

for to swing as the Nat King Cole Three.

Ol' King Cole swang with natural soul,

with nematic control swang he.

He snared a bass man

and netted a guitar —

now Nat nails down the 88 keys.

Mister Bass Man, he had the know-how

and the string man more knowing was he.

Add the King's nimble flair —

'twas a swinging affair —

with Nat Cole and his numinous three.

O away an oasis ailes, an oboe

bows below both boroughs blows! because

cold, cold oak seek ēco key cozy soul owed.

Odious ode! dough-dee-doed a doughy yodel oh-oh! oy!

Oedipus so easy eats eons, eels a week. eel! eel! eel! awful.

Photos of folk off a foggy flu, flow froze for froggy fog, ogling

golden ogres or groggy gophers on goals gone gooey who?

How hoopin' hogs hold hour hooligan hosts ahoy, ions boy!

Eye only on onions, aye-aye! aisle oil only Ohio Why — (Oh?) No go!

Joe joggle Jo Jabbo? No Joe! Jo Jo jovial j-j jokey Jones. Jowls, owls

on okra, corn OK. Coffee kayos kooks cookoo oaks, oakey-cokey cacao coin-oinking

      Koalas. Olé!

Lo O'Leary's lore lures lonely only loyal oily Olympians. Oh me!

Omit my meow mow molten moany moldy me mostly mocha omissions

on no noon. New oat known own noun neo noisy no nosy nay nozzle Ooop!

Ooh oozy oomph. Ow! Oompah varoom! "Oolong of oodles," opined Ophelia

portly opened pour posted au pair opposite polly-opals pro quo quakkis

oak Quintana Roo quoth roccoco cue co-wrote,

      "Our round droll groom drools orange o'er trolls to trounce known knolls,"

where Homer wrote, "Nor ornament, nor orthodoxy, nor ornithology.

Or-Or-Or-Or-Ornette!!"

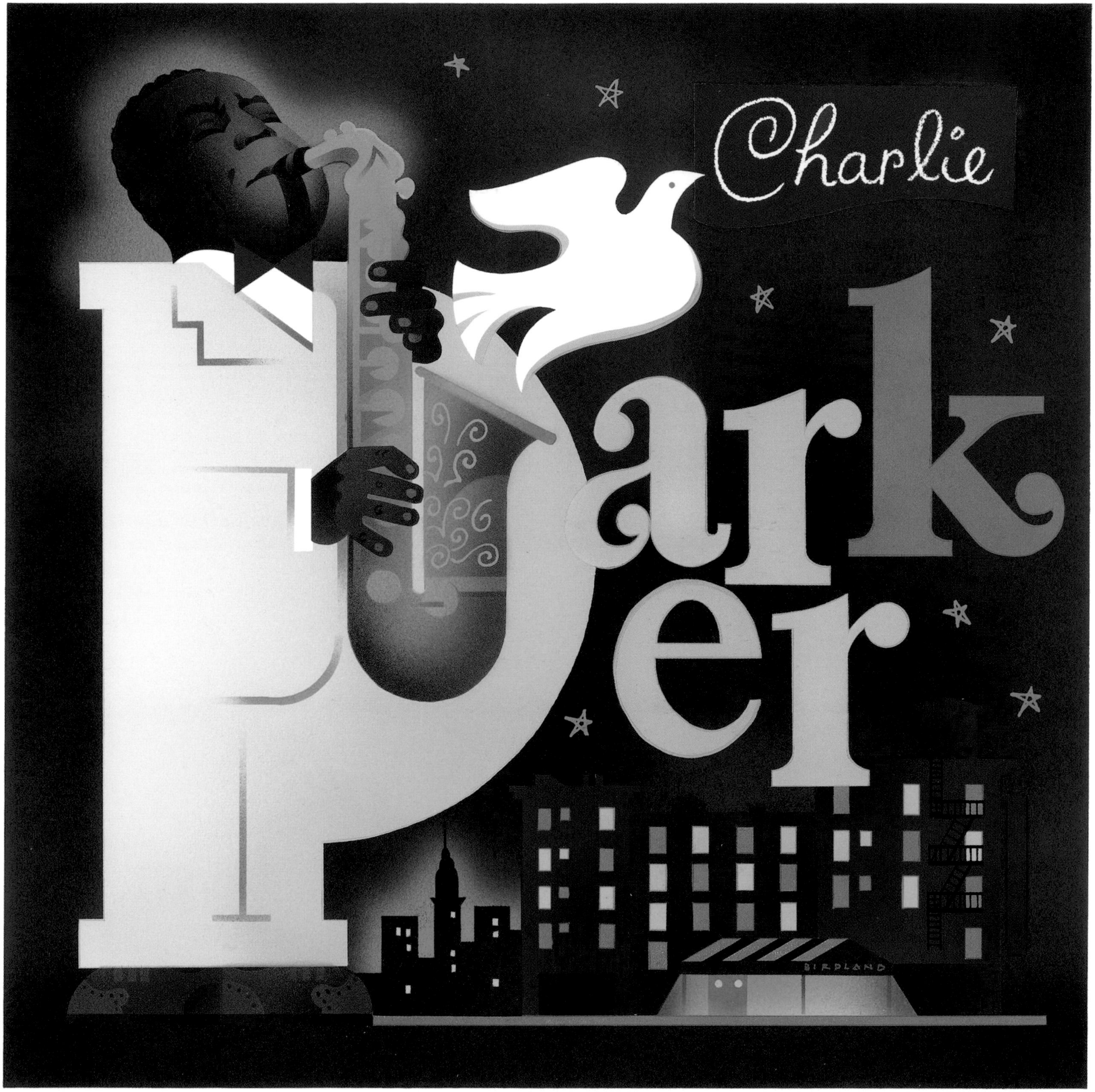

Charlie
Parker
BIRDLAND

Charlie Parker plays perfect music.

Pithy passionate phrases proclaim peace, pride, pain.

Parker's provocative personal life appalls the public.

Perhaps he'll prop up puerile popular pieces with plausible psychological possibilities.

Pithy passionate phrases proclaim pain, pride, peace, and pleasure.

Picture Parker playing, posture perfect, sloppily sporting an unpressed pinstripe suit and crumply polka dot tie.

Perhaps he'll punctuate popular pieces with prestissimo psychological possibilities.

Probably, Parker will apply a heaping portion of the blues to inspirit impassive patrons.

Parker plays with perfect posture, sporting a sloppy pinstripe suit and pink paisley tie.

Each pitiless note pierces the prejudiced presumptions of poseurs and pontificators.

Presently, Parker will apply heaping portions of blues to inspire impassive patrons.

This Prometheus of improvisation pours pure perception from a well-practiced pipe of curved gold.

Each pitiless note pierces the prejudiced presumptions of postulating poseurs and pontificating pundits.

Parker is the preeminent poet and pied-pipering prophet of pre-primitive, post-modern philosophy.

This Prometheus pours pure perception from a well-practiced pipe of curved gold.

Persistent preacher of positivity, Parker purges pessimism with a pitter-patter of piquant percussive pearls.

Parker is the preeminent poet and pied piper prophetic of pre-primitive, post-modern philosophy.

A phenomena, a paradox, priest and pagan, participant and pariah, prince and peasant, Parker presents an impenetrable puzzle.

Persistent preacher of positivity, Parker purges pessimism with a peppy parade of polished percussive pearls.

The people put Parker on a pedestal, praising his prodigious aptitude and protean prowess.

A phenomena, a paradox, pious priest and peccant pagan, participant and pariah, prince and peasant, Parker, the person, poses an impenetrable problem.

Peerless improviser of unprecedented profundity purposefully persecuted by a corrupted press.

Still, the people put Parker on a pedestal, praising his prodigious aptitude and pioneering approach.

And the passage of time has proven that Parker's playing, the pinnacle of spontaneous improvisation, prevails.

Milt Jackson is a quick study.

On quirky complicated arrangements, he

Doesn't even require music.

Ever check out Milt's vibe on quarrelsome tunes?

Rest easy. He has no qualms about navigating a quagmire of querulous

Nonnegotiable harmonies. Milt'll just quote some blues.

John Lewis is quality control.

A piano man of exquisite taste, quite

Zealous in his quest for refined ensemble work. He

Zooms in for the most judicious quantity of soul nuggets.

Query bassist Percy Heath about quadruple time, but

Under no circumstances quiz him about the

Absolute authority of his quarter notes.

Rather than upset Percy, request talk-time with

The quantumly qualified Connie Kay. What a quorum! The MJQ.

Equal partners, equable swingers with quiet intensity.

This quadrumvirate just makes music jump! Questions?

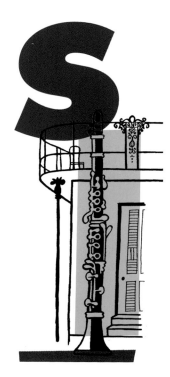

Still Sidney shouts, salty sweetness screaming sassy sanguine sounds on

    sappy songs, scalding scooped scales with the superscientific sashaying of a

    seer; savvy sacrilegious saliferous satyr sacrificing safety to supremely

    sing solemn spirituals on a scorching soprano saxophone. Sagacious

    saint of sacrosanct sayings, sardonic sultan of sarcasm and of scrappy

    satirical sounds swung slowly or savagely scandalizing shallow society

    softies with soaring scarlet scherzos, so scholarly, so scintillating,

    so scurrilously so! Scrupulous scrooge of scuttlebutt sausaged through a

    smoldering black stick, seamless seamster of searing, seditious, seismic

    statements. Self-asserted, self-fulfilled, self-perpetuated,

    self-realized, *selfless* signatory of the sensuous semitone, slipping and

    sliding softly like a sneaky senior senator selling sensitive secrets.

Still Sidney shouts sepia short stories with serious and silly serpentine

    sentences, sapphire sentiments set in stone, seventh-day soliloquies set

    aside. Striving for Seven Seals severity or swashbuckling sforzandos, he

    shakes the shadows of sharps and shatters shammers with sharp-tongued,

    sharp-witted, sharp-sighted senses of shaman. His unsheathed saber of

    a sound shields the shell-shocked, shelters the sheepish, and shores up

    the shellacked. Sans sheet music, Sidney shimmies and shivers

    all over schmaltz to shock a sterile shindig with some stellar shoot-'em-up

    solos. So he's short. So short-haired as to be shining but never so-so.

    Short-fused and short-spoken too, sometimes. When Sidney straight-up says

    "Shut up, son," self-assuredly shrug, spurn his shrewishness,

    and shuffle on south, or shush him, stay, and sidle

    up to the sax stand to see his sibilant, sighing, soul-sifting signature:

    sanctified siren songs singeing silence with silken silvery slivers of sizzling

    sixteenth notes silhouetting sinuous sinful slurs.

Still Sidney skewers skeptics with such skill, skipping from style to style.

A skipper of skiffle, some say savior of skunky, smelly, signifying southern
sax sounds slashing slant-wise through sophistication, slop, and slumber,
singing sorrowfully of slavery and the slaughterhouse and so so much
sickness and the slick and sleazy who slinkily slide the slippery
slopes of slimy slobber. Oh Sidney! Super sovereign of sonic speed
and of serving up slushy slow drags so successfully as to smack the
smile-side off a smarmy smooth smart-aleck's smirk. Sidney'll do
all the smirking then send smothering smoke smooching through a
simmering black stick to snap the spell surrounding a snake-bit
sufferer. Sneer, snicker, or sneeze, but stop sniping. Sidney's no snitch
or sneaky Pete. He snatch sadness by the snout and serve up a satiating
sermon of salvation, then socialize the same with soaked or sober.
So suave and so social, so successful without soft-shoeing or selling out,
a soldier of sock-cymbal swing solidly singing saucy solfeggio, sending
sonorous somersaults into the stratosphere. A songwriter, a sonneteer,
a sorcerer of sorghum sonatas so sweetly sung. Sung sotto voce, sung
seriously, sung with soul yes, with soul and souse. A sound swathed in
souse and spare-ribs sauce, sparkling in specialness, scouring the
spectrum of space-time but still spilling with spit and spice into the
spirit-sphere splintering and spluttering splendiferously.

Still Sidney shouts and spouts sporting songs, songs of spring and Spanish
songs, splashy, spontaneous, on-the-spot songs. Sometimes he squeaks
and squawks, squooshing and squeezing spunky staccato stammerings
that saddle the sparky stars. Sometimes standoffish stars set the
standards of style. Sometimes . . . Sidney stands fast. He stands up to
starch the static stitching from a song by stealth, stealing the sting

from stereotypes and stamping the swagger out of standard-bearers while sabotaging the staminiferous, staid, stock statesman of stuffiness through startling standing-ovation singsong statements on a shiny saber said to be a soprano saxophone. Said to be steely, steadfast and sterling in the service of stiff-arming the stuck-up with stentorian seriousness. Or stingy, stalwart, and stiff-chinned about scraping the stardust off of some Stone-Aged standard and spangling the sky with syrup. Said to be smitteningly soft and snowy but still stringent, strident, and stridulous so as to slap one's senses however strong-minded or stubborn into a stuttering stupor of satisfied submission. Some of Sidney's stunts — subito subdivision of the swing into subatomic spools of sublime satin, subliminal sharing of substantial subcultural subjects through the superconscious subdominant — subsist in substantiating the supremacy of spiraling, super serene, sweltering soul. Such soul as subverts selfish suckers and subterranean backstabbers by suffocation with sheets of and showerings of sugar. Sidney's something, boy! Sometimes sulky or sullen, but seldom sunken or sullied. Never stopped! Super-eminent superhero of sultry, supple, succinct summons to stomp a schottische sundance, to sunbathe in a superior sound, to supersaturate the soul in the supernal style of a superstitious, super-sensitive, supernatural supremo of sustained surprise.

Still Sidney shouts no surrender but swaggers of soaring swallows, sweats of summer swamp fever, swoops of swan's sweeping dive. Under the swarthy strain of suspicion, he swings and sways on sax and smoldering stick of ebony. He, Sidney, synthesizes a southern system of speaking into a superb symphony of syncopation. I swear.

Rollins's robust style radiates roundness.

On raucous rhythms or sweet romances

Sonny resoundingly responds,

Raging rhapsodic on regular songs

Rendered swimmingly. Rollins rarely rests.

His rebellious ragging sparkplugged rebop.

Sonny reinvigorates rituals.

Strong in rejoicing, right rooted in risk,

Rollins's robust style radiates roundness.

Refusing to rust or rot in sameness,

Sonny refurbishes rickety riffs.

Rangy runner romping sheer razor's rim.

Raspy rambles raise shivers 'round the room.

Redolent of re-refined sauciness,

Rollins's robust style radiates roundness.

Tonight ...

there's Thelonious

ticklin'

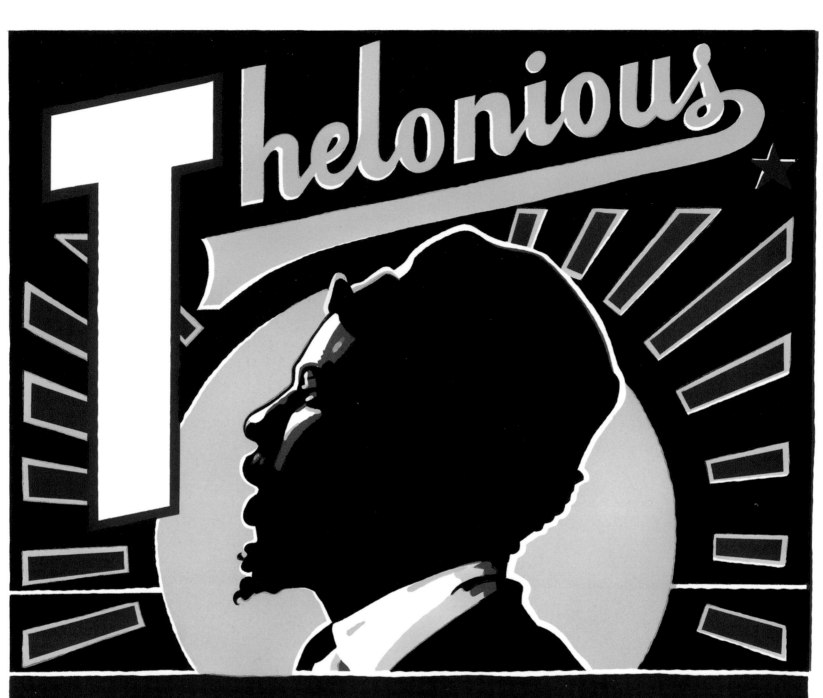

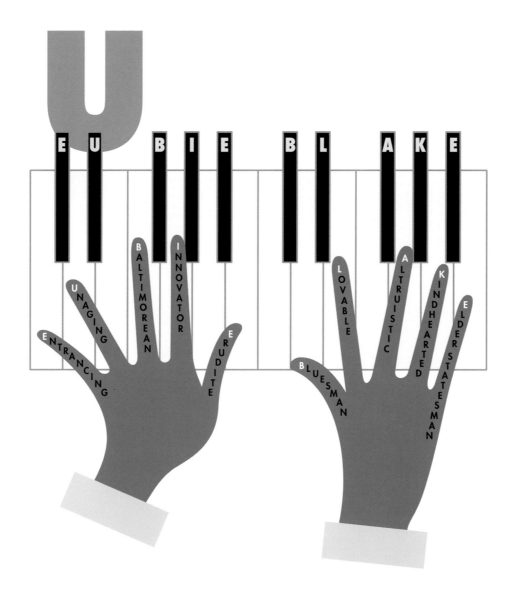

Everybody's **u**rgent 'bout **i**nterviewing Eubie. **B**ut **l**et **a** **k**ing **e**at.

A vital, vast, vivacious, vernal voice

with violet, velvet virtues sings to me.

Some hear a vaunted vixen's soul rejoice

in vain. I hear the voice of verity.

In vowel and verb and verse and sweet refrain,

her vestal vexing vigorates my soul

and voids the vagrant values that restrain

my heart. She sings; I vanquish all control —

in vanquishing, so validate the view

that loss is gain, and vouch to venerate

with vengeance what I love. Her voodooed stew

of varied windswept songs I gladly taste.

Let virgin ears and veterans who knew

her testify, "Sarah Vaughan, we love you."

In the wrinkling wind of winter, me and my wonderful wife Wilma walked up to this weird, wigged-out hole in the wall. We wanted to witness who we were told was the most noteworthy piano wizard in the whole wide world. Man, we just couldn't wait. . . . But we did. Was about a week to get in that Wednesday night and I was wonderin' whether me and my woman would just write it off and walk on away. Man, who wanted to wait around outside of some wormy watering hole with his wife? Wall to wall wastrels wetting their whiskers with waves of cheap wine, whiskey, and wodka. . . . We did! Wellsuh, some kinda way we wriggled our way into this wasted joint. *Wow! What a welcome.* We watch every-one everywhere at once. There he was! The woolly wildman, wildman wolf-jawed wizard. Whack-whump-whomp! Whack-whump-whomp! His left hand was working watchdog in the wilderness. The wood-stained walls was weepin'. Man, this cat was a workman! A well-tailored heavyweight who had willfully wept in the woodshed so unwaveringly through the waning hours that walloping the Weltanschauung out of a piano was an act of holy worship, of waging war on the wing. Looky here, with the wily wolf-jaw waxing and whomping, this wasn't noplace for a wilterin' wallflower. Was time for waggin' brother, waggin' a tailfeather. Man, me and my Wilma wondered, just *who* is this wondrous, witch-of-a-woolly-mammoth wizard of the black and whites? Some fella says, "Waller, man. Fats Waller." Wellsuh, me and Wilma winks at each other and walks away whisperin', "Waller was well worth the wait."

Let's visit with a boy of six.

He extracts songs by ear.

He executes cute piano tricks.

Excitedly we cheer.

His folks fix up a piano class.

Some expert way in town.

The boy excels at every task,

But reading knocks him down.

His parents nix his studies now,

A punishment extreme.

At fifteen, disks of jazz arouse

Expression of his dream.

He blows a cornet extra long

Vexing his mom and dad.

Expelled to war school from his home,

He exits blowing jazz.

Escaping war school he expands

This complex native sound.

He mixes with the brown-skinned bands,

Explores this jazz he's found.

He exalts in lyric sweetness,

Excites on zesty jumps,

Exhibits exclusive features,

Exudes that umpty-umph!

He travels on extensively,

Exports the jazz solo.

His records are exemplary,

But whiskey lays him low.

Exhausted, he goes home to fix

What tattered soul he has.

His folks reject his life's love. Bix,

He exits blowing jazz.

Could the yawning cry

of happy yattering sax perhaps be

Lester Wildebeest Young?

Yeah y'all! (you yell at yourself)

He spins glittery blue yarns with golden yellow.

Zoom! He flies
international skies
in a crazy disguise.
The maddeningly wise
super-size
genius with bad ties.
Watch him alphabetize,
realize,
and energize
a bebop that fiery-flies
without compromise
to capsize
to *Zap!*
the claptrap
of silly, silly yap
that straps
us into zoned-out maps
of boring zero.
So when you're low
or just so-so,
he'll bestow
blazing lines for your ego.
Streaky notes that yo-yo
and to and fro flow
from lindy hop to go-go.

He's a high-wire hero
with more tricks in his bag;
phrases that zigzag
a zinjanthropus rag
some hilarious gag
about a useless wag
or a nincompoop nag
who's always a drag.
Who's who?
He's country, that's true,
but New York new, too.
He's a trip to the zoo,
Carolina stew,
Loosianna catfish and Texas barbecue,
a how-do-you-do
when you want to boo-hoo.
A baby's goo-goo
or a tasted taboo.
He's the cluck of a cuckoo
at the final clue.
A ride on a choo-choo.
A paid IOU.
The generous guru
of southern fried hoo-doo.
Who knew
that he blew
a kazoo
of bamboo
or a didjeridoo
that makes zebras moo?

He's brilliant and zany,
all kinds of brainy.
You know what he has?
It's called pizzazz.
That's what makes his style of jazz.
Even when he snoozes,
his snoring oozes
the dreams of muses.
Now don't go fanaticizing,
idolizing, aggrandizing,
or even analyzing.
Go about recognizing
him for fertilizing
a civilizing
style back then
that's come 'round again.
Besides, who knows when
he became a master of Zen?
Sound the trumpet *and* say amen —
an eleven on the scale of one to ten.
Be you friend, foe, or kin,
always ready with a, "Man, how you been?"
Why he's Daniel in the lion's den,
a leader of men
who's always busy,
cheeks poked out and hair all frizzy.
Ditsy, zany, loose, or is he?
Now don't you go gettin' all up in a tizzy.
You know I'm talking about
the zenith, the alpha, Dizzy.

BIOGRAPHICAL SKETCHES by Phil Schaap

LOUIS ARMSTRONG | 1901–1971

Louis "Satchmo" Armstrong, trumpeter and vocalist from New Orleans, is the most influential musician of the twentieth century. Armstrong's virtuosity, his trailblazing of improvisation and swing, and his vocal style still prove Pops is tops.

As a child, Louis displayed musical interest and talent, but it was a stint in reform school that led to his first music lessons. He became a professional musician in the early New Orleans jazz scene, and his pioneering mentor, King Oliver, eventually brought him north to join the King's Creole Jazz Band in Chicago.

In 1924, Fletcher Henderson, the most prominent jazz big-band leader, brought Satchmo to New York City, where and when Armstrong began to teach the world how to swing. Next Armstrong got a record contract and started making the seminal Hot Five recordings.

Until the late 1940s, Armstrong would both front and form big bands. Toward the end of the Swing Era, he returned to New Orleans and the glories of the Hot Fives. The success of these traditional jazz engagements led in 1947 to the formation of his last band.

By instrumentation a traditional jazz group, Louis Armstrong and the All-Stars performed a varied repertoire. Hits such as "Mack the Knife" and "What a Wonderful World" occasionally displaced Elvis Presley and the Beatles from the top rungs of the pop charts. During this period, "Ambassador Satch" was one of the most beloved American figures and often was sent abroad by the United States on goodwill tours.

COUNT BASIE | 1904–1984

In his teens, pianist William "Count" Basie moved to Harlem and became a protégé of Fats Waller. Young Basie soon became a vital cog in the road companies that played the black vaudeville circuit. But he fell in love in Tulsa at the age of twenty-one, and it lasted a lifetime. His love was for the southwestern style of jazz and blues and for the musicians who played it. Those musicians, in turn, fell in love with Count Basie's style.

Basie, a New Jersey native, had blended the two primary schools of jazz piano: Earl Hines's approach, with its horn-like phrasing, and the style known as Stride. By 1929, he was playing in Bennie Moten's Kansas City Orchestra. At the start of the Swing Era, Basie got a chance to create his own big band. He built it uniquely, starting with the rhythm section and featuring dueling tenor saxophones.

The Count Basie Orchestra came north in 1936 and, taking Southwestern Swing on the road, soon was as successful as any band in the country. Known now as Kansas City Jazz, Southwestern Swing first became a national, then an international, sensation.

Count Basie's big band lasted until the era ended in 1950. For two years Count led a small group, but in 1951 he took a chance and reformed his band. That second, "New Testament" Count Basie Orchestra was *the* surprise of pop music — it even had rock 'n' roll hits. The Count's success story continues; his orchestra still plays K.C. Jazz to this day.

JOHN COLTRANE | 1926–1967

John Coltrane on tenor saxophone, as well as soprano, dominated jazz during the early and middle 1960s. Trane, however, was a late bloomer. Although he was a musician from an early age, he had entered his thirties before he exhibited one of the most awesome techniques ever encountered in music history.

John William Coltrane studied clarinet as a child and concentrated on alto saxophone during adolescence and his earliest professional work. Trane was determined to play like Charlie Parker, but long before he completed this Herculean task, he had changed to tenor sax.

From 1949 to 1951, John Coltrane worked with Dizzy Gillespie. It almost was his only big-time exposure until Miles Davis selected Trane as a charter member of his classic quintet in 1955. From that point on, John Coltrane was in the limelight.

Toward the end of the 1950s, Coltrane envisioned his own future: he would lead a quartet. The music of the John Coltrane Quartet offered the leader's "sheets of sound" display of technique, but also a leaner and more melodic approach influenced by the modal music he had been part of with Miles Davis.

In subsequent years, Coltrane continued to experiment with and develop his musical style, which eventually offered a spiritual focus, as well as intense displays of raw Free Jazz or "high-energy" improvisation. His popularity grew exponentially regardless of his stylistic changes, and he was one of the few jazz heroes to young people during the 1960s. His popularity continues to grow, even with the youth of today.

MILES DAVIS | 1926–1991

Miles Davis, a trumpeter, was a primary figure in BeBop and the essential trailblazer in Cool Jazz, Hard Bop, Modal Jazz, and Fusion. A pop star during his lifetime, he remains one of the few universally recognized jazz musicians.

Miles Dewey Davis III hailed from a family that had become well-to-do in the brief but exceptional period of opportunities for African Americans following the Civil War. He followed jazz as a listener until his father gave him a trumpet for his thirteenth birthday. He then studied with the best brass teachers in St. Louis, Missouri, and emerged a professional at age fifteen.

Davis was enamored of Charlie Parker's and Dizzy Gillespie's BeBop breakthrough, and his primary early gig was in the "golden era" Charlie Parker Quintet. Next Davis created an innovative and incredibly influential ensemble now known as the Birth of the Cool. This began of a series of Miles Davis–led bands, each of which presented a fresh approach to jazz, dominating the new idiom they had created.

In 1955, Davis's Hard Bop Classic Quintet featured John Coltrane. By 1958, his sextet had introduced Modal Jazz. A subsequent quintet did not create a named new style but was nevertheless influential. And in the late 1960s, a different Davis ensemble used electronic instruments and fused rock 'n' roll to jazz.

Miles was never sentimental or reverential about his own legacy—his last hurrah, a 1991 appearance at Montreux, surprisingly was a return to the remarkable orchestral music Gil Evans wrote for him in the 1950s.

DUKE ELLINGTON | 1899–1974

Duke Ellington played piano, but the orchestra was his real instrument. And Duke used it to play his music, the most important compositions in all of jazz.

Edward Kennedy "Duke" Ellington was brought up in an elegant home with many niceties, including piano lessons. Initially, he was indifferent to music, but during his adolescence, he became passionate about it and soon was leading a jazz band.

That unit, transplanted to New York City, brought him to prominence. Their opening at the Cotton Club on December 4, 1927, was a pivotal gig that provided a forum for Duke to perform and compose. Ellington's music now bore his stamp of identity and genius.

The Duke Ellington Orchestra had numerous successes, while Duke also made movies and did international touring. Greater glory came in the Swing Era with the addition to his orchestra of Billy Strayhorn, who brought new music to the maestro; Jimmie Blanton, an exceptional bassist whose genius created a soloing role for the instrument; and Ben Webster, who was a mastermind on the newly important tenor saxophone.

After the Swing Era, Duke Ellington's Orchestra could be said to have triumphed simply by existing, as economics caused all the other big bands to fold. Even Duke had troubles, among them a criticism that the maestro was a has-been. Ellington answered such jibes with a resolving triumph at the 1956 Newport Jazz Festival. Thereafter, no one challenged the maestro's supremacy, and he continued performing until the end of his life.

ELLA FITZGERALD | 1917–1996

Ella Fitzgerald was blessed with a voice that knew few boundaries. She used her gift to sing jazz. Nobody has out-sung her or out-swung her to date.

During the Great Depression, "the First Lady of Song" came to Harlem with no money and no place to stay. Ella entered Harlem's famed amateur contests, including the still extant one at the Apollo. She won them all and launched her career.

Her big break was singing with the Chick Webb Orchestra, the house band at the legendary Savoy Ballroom. In 1938, they had a number-one record: *A-Tisket, A-Tasket*. When Webb died the next year, Ella took over. She led the band for more than three years, thereafter working in far smaller units.

During the mid-1940s, Ella Fitzgerald had a series of hits for the Decca label, several of which helped popularize BeBop. She soon was touring with Jazz at the Philharmonic, and by the mid-1950s, Ella was far and away JATP's superstar.

The producer of JATP, Norman Granz, became her manager and record producer. For his Verve label, Ella Fitzgerald created a series of songbook albums that are considered the finest of all such attempts. She also made three albums with Louis Armstrong and a series of "travelogue" LPs.

Even when her vocal cords and strength started to ebb, Ella Fitzgerald remained jazz's best-known singer and its most in-demand concert artist.

GERRY MULLIGAN | 1927–1996

"Jeru" just might be the most significant figure in the Cool School of jazz. Mulligan combined the rhythmic relaxation heard in the Swing Era and coupled it to the emphasis on technique and display of harmonic knowledge common to BeBop. That's Cool Jazz, and Gerry was cool.

Gerry "Jeru" Mulligan came of age in the Swing Era, and when he was still a teenager, he placed his arrangements in name big bands such as Gene Krupa's. When those big bands disappeared, Mulligan was forced to concentrate on his playing. By 1948, Gerry Mulligan was a baritone saxophonist whose style reflected Lester Young and Charlie Parker.

Still wishing to write music, Jeru hooked up with Miles Davis, who had organized a midsize ensemble that gave several arranger-composers an outlet. Mulligan both played in and wrote for Davis's Birth of the Cool nonet. By the time the Cool School was born, Gerry Mulligan was leading the way.

Jeru moved to California in 1951 and soon formed a quartet that made hit records for the Pacific label. (This largely explains why Cool is also called West Coast Jazz.) He longed for a big band and launched an influential one in 1960, the Gerry Mulligan Concert Jazz Band. Although later he briefly would have another big band, his first orchestra foundered for economic reasons, and by 1968, Mulligan was playing with Dave Brubeck. He also led smaller groups and wrote large-scale works for special occasions and others' ensembles.

COLEMAN HAWKINS | 1904–1969

A trailblazer from the 1910s until the 1960s, Coleman Hawkins was jazz's first tenor saxophonist. His virtuosity led others to take up the instrument and also to its dominance among the horns, and his rhapsodic playing perfected the ballad concept in jazz.

Around age eleven, young Coleman Randolph Hawkins heard an all-saxophone band that sealed his destiny. Five years later, he was the best performer in Missouri on this still-new instrument. When most jazz players' spontaneity came only in ad-libbed breaks, "Hawk" was the complete package, a "get-off man" who could create a fully improvised chorus.

At seventeen, he joined Mamie Smith's Jazz Hounds. During a long gig in the Big Apple, Hawk discovered that he was the best saxophonist around, so he quit Smith and became NYC's top freelancer. In 1923, Fletcher Henderson, who had been using Hawkins, started a big band, and thus "Bean" became a charter member of the pioneering Fletcher Henderson Orchestra and the ensemble's most important soloist.

Hawkins went to Europe in 1934 and was the leading jazz performer on the continent until World War II. America now called jazz its pop music, and Hawk's first record upon his return, *Body and Soul,* became his biggest hit.

Next he half-heartedly launched a Swing Era big band, but fell in love with BeBop. He became both a father figure to and a co-conspirator in the BeBop revolution and was influential in many subsequent jazz "adventures." Traditional, mainstream, and avant-garde musicians revered him to the end.

ART BLAKEY (Abdullah Ibn Buhaina) | 1919–1990

Art Blakey, percussionist and bandleader, presented the most hard-hitting, soulful jazz music of the second half of the twentieth century. Blakey became the primary member of the generation that took on the challenge of retaining BeBop's innovations while restoring the earthy, blues-filled, folk elements of jazz's early times — without spoiling either. Buhaina, as Blakey is sometimes known, was successful; his music is known as Hard Bop.

Born Art Blakey, Abdullah Ibn Buhaina was determined to avoid the harsh labor of Pittsburgh's steel mills by playing music professionally. Young Buhaina's drumming derived much from Chick Webb's fervent style.

Art Blakey was "discovered" by Fletcher Henderson, jazz's pioneering big-band leader. Other prominent early work included three years in Billy Eckstine's orchestra, the prototype of big-band BeBop, and a first orchestra of his own.

The hugely important jazz record company Blue Note favored Art Blakey over all other drummers. Art selected a live setting for his recordings, the original Birdland club, and hired young talent whom he could direct in playing his musical vision. The thirty-four-year-old Art Blakey even announced on the record that the balance of his career would follow this formula: he would forever surround himself with young talent.

Buhaina was true to his word. Soon, he was to lead the most long-lived band of Hard Bop, Art Blakey and the Jazz Messengers. Every few years, Art would renew his ensemble with the next generation's talent. (At the start of the 1980s, the trumpeter was a teenage Wynton Marsalis.)

JELLY ROLL MORTON | ca. 1890–1941

Jelly Roll Morton, a New Orleans Jazz pioneer, was the music's first great composer. Jelly Roll Morton the pianist also was vital to the emergence of jazz, as he was one of the new music's greatest ad-libbers. Morton could sing well, and his arranging also showcased his genius. Beyond the actual notes, Jelly's scores were the beginning of a system that defined the ensemble and solo roles in a jazz band.

Jelly Roll Morton's real first name was Ferdinand, his middle Joseph, and he went by more than one family name. The specifics of his musical training are unknown, but he emerged in his mid-teens a fully trained and accomplished pianist whose performances displayed a full grasp of Buddy Bolden's breakthroughs.

Unlike the other New Orleans Jazz pioneers, who stayed in New Orleans until the 1910s or 1920s, Jelly Roll left early, taking the message of jazz to many places where it was heard for the first time and embraced.

His great talent and prominence in jazz led the prestigious Victor label to sign him. From 1926 to 1930, Jelly made his most influential and musically significant records, the Jelly Roll Morton Red Hot Peppers tracks.

The Great Depression ended Morton's success. Toward the end of the 1930s, Jelly Roll was living in Washington, D.C., and running a second-rate nightclub. But curiosity arose during the Swing Era about where jazz had come from, and this led to a revival of early New Orleans Jazz and Jelly Roll himself.

KING OLIVER | 1885–1938

King Oliver is assured a place in history because he was Louis Armstrong's mentor. But he earns his own spot in the jazz pantheon by his music. Oliver's wizardry was essential to the emergence of jazz. His early solo work is the prototype: King's improvisations replace the song's melody but follow its form. It's still done that way today.

Playing the trumpet-like cornet, Joe "King" Oliver became the leading figure in New Orleans, the music's birthplace, in the early 1910s. Oliver then went on to become the most important jazzman in Chicago, where he founded his own band.

King Oliver's Creole Jazz Band is the most important of the early bands. They represent the all-ensemble tradition at its peak, with several key members exhibiting the then-new advent to jazz, the solo. No fewer than four members of this septet (later octet) were certifiable geniuses: the King himself; his protégé Louis Armstrong; and the Doddses—Johnny on clarinet and Baby on drums. Their many recordings allow us still to know their greatness.

Great they were, but King Oliver switched to a big band by the mid-1920s. Oliver, ever the trailblazer, saw that the dance orchestra was more suitable for implementing the solo.

King Oliver led his orchestra into the mid-1930s, but the Great Depression and some individual bad breaks left him working twelve hours a day as a janitor. His letters to his sister from this period reveal a bit of artistry with words and a Job-like patience in accepting adversity.

BILLIE HOLIDAY | 1915–1959

Although Billie Holiday lacked the awe-inspiring elements expected in singers, she is *the* jazz vocalist. Her definitive emotional power even reaches the hearts of many who appreciate her alone among jazz performers.

Billie Holiday, or "Lady Day" as she was known, was born Elinore Harris (later Eleanora Fagan). She renamed herself "Billie" after motion picture star Billie Dove and chose the surname of her biological father, jazz plectorist Clarence Holiday.

Among young Lady Day's favorite recordings were Louis Armstrong's, and his singing is the root of her style. By the early 1930s, she was singing professionally in New York. Her concept was remarkably relaxed, and she was in the forefront of the rhythmic revolutionaries of the Swing Era who elasticized jazz's beat.

Talent scout and producer John Hammond hired her for a series of records that would change the way a jazz song's words were presented. Lady Day's vocal delivery was one in a string of solos, otherwise made by instrumentalists, in a miniature jam now known as "the swing song tradition." Afterward she became a headline cabaret singer and, as a celebrity chanteuse, debuted at Carnegie Hall and appeared in a film with Louis Armstrong.

At superstardom's zenith, Billie Holiday's heroin addiction caught up with her. Fame continued, but notoriety now included details of drug busts and missed engagements. But she hit pockets of consistent performance in her later years, and most of her last records happily returned to the swing song tradition.

CHARLES MINGUS | 1922–1979

Charles Mingus, a rare illustration of the jazz musician in control of the business side of his art, called his band Charles Mingus's Jazz Workshop. He created it to provide a forum to perform his compositions and showcase his bass, an instrument he played with exceedingly rare virtuosity. He directed his bands in a manner best described as "over the top." Charles Mingus, however, always displayed the deepest dedication to jazz and a profound understanding of its music.

Raised in Los Angeles, Mingus studied both trombone and cello before settling on the string bass. He worked hard to develop his technique and was rewarded by big gigs in his early career. But he was motivated to do more than make other people's bands sound better: he wanted to lead his own orchestra, featuring his own compositions. Mingus felt he had the potential to be the next Duke Ellington and dubbed himself "Baron." The genius was there but not the following, and his early career failed.

Next Mingus tried the more traditional route of prominent membership in successful bands, playing for two great jazz vibraphonists, Lionel Hampton and Red Norvo. With his reputation grown, he returned to his own course, highlighted by forming his own record company, Debut. Soon he was a highly regarded bandleader.

Performances by Charles Mingus's Jazz Workshop sometimes resembled rehearsals. They were, nevertheless, effective presentations that allowed Mingus, the conductor, to get his music played well. The group fell victim to jazz's economic downturn in the 1960s. Mingus made no records for more than five years, but he did enjoy a huge renaissance in the 1970s.

NAT KING COLE | 1917–1965

If Nat King Cole had never opened his mouth, he would still be an all-time jazz great based on his marvelous piano stylings. But of course Nat King Cole did sing, and his consummate artistry as a pop singer made him a superstar.

Nathaniel Adams Coles, whose family was part of the black migration northward, was raised in Chicago. By his mid-teens, Coles was an important jazz pianist who often worked as a leader. A turning point occurred when he played in a road company production of Sissle & Blake's *Shuffle Along*. It took Nat Coles to Los Angeles, where he formed an innovative trio of piano, bass, and electric guitar. It was called the King Cole Trio, and he became Nat "King" Cole.

The King Cole Trio was a jazz unit, and Nat King Cole became the top jazz pianist on the West Coast. The trio often featured novelty vocals and occasional solo singing by the leader. In 1943, they had their first block-buster hit with "Straighten Up and Fly Right." Three years later, the hit was "The Christmas Song," and the character of Nat King Cole's career changed forever. He became a full-time singer and pop star.

Nat King Cole appeared in motion pictures and had his own television show, a first for an African American. During the 1950s and early 1960s, Cole would occasionally display his continuing jazz prowess.

ORNETTE COLEMAN | 1930–

Ornette Coleman, primarily an alto saxophonist, created a new approach called Free Jazz, perhaps the most renegade of various attempts to free improvisers from the clichés of BeBop's chord-running solos.

Free Jazz de-emphasized Western diatonic music, with fixed pitches often taking a back seat to sounds—strange sounds, said most critics, yet Coleman's dismissal of chords propelled players toward a melodic approach. Both as a player and as a gifted composer, Coleman demonstrated the lyrical potential of his own concept.

Ornette's real mentors were the blues, as well as, surprisingly, Charlie Parker's BeBop. However, instead of going back to the work song and the blues, Coleman suggested that the player make the actual sound of laborers' anguish—crying on one's instrument rather then playing songs about tears. In this he trumped Hard Bop, which emphasized jazz's roots.

Coleman found some young California musicians who became not just followers but members of an Ornette Coleman group that played his Free Jazz, receiving record contracts and major performance opportunities.

In the 1960s, Coleman moved to Europe. There he wrote Third Stream compositions, blending jazz and classical. Ornette's return in 1967 found him presenting jazz in his own home, a loft in Lower Manhattan. This launched Loft Jazz, still in vogue today.

Out of the common musical language of jazz, Coleman created a new style so abstract to its foundation that many cannot hear the connection. Yet this feat testifies to his individuality and genius. Ornette Coleman remains the patron saint of avant-garde music.

CHARLIE PARKER | 1920–1955

Charlie Parker, displaying virtuosity and a new sense of the beat, improvised strings of notes that revealed a deep knowledge and insight into harmony. Parker's style is the core of BeBop, the new jazz of the 1940s and the style that dominates to this day.

Charles Parker Jr. could be called a musical late bloomer. Once he decided to become an alto saxophonist, however, the teenage Parker became highly regarded in the Kansas City jazz scene.

Parker hoboed his way north to Chicago, then to New York, where he hardly worked but participated in jam sessions. While improvising on "Cherokee," he had the revelation that led to BeBop.

Charlie Parker returned to Kansas City in 1940 and joined the Jay McShann Orchestra, where he was given the nickname "Yardbird," or "Bird." During this period, Parker met Dizzy Gillespie. Their partnership allowed BeBop to mature into a fully realized new music.

After 1946, Charlie Parker and Dizzy Gillespie separately continued their BeBop campaign. Bird formed the Charlie Parker Quintet, featuring Miles Davis and Max Roach and known as his Golden Era BeBop Five. After his hit "Just Friends," Parker created a new band, Charlie Parker with Strings.

Later, Bird began to experiment, testing the waters of the Third Stream, a blend of classical and jazz, and performing on a plastic saxophone. He hoped for another breakthrough of the magnitude of BeBop. Sadly, his heroin addiction and possibly depression over the death of his daughter ended his life prematurely.

MODERN JAZZ QUARTET | Founded 1952

When Dizzy Gillespie had his BeBop Big Band in the mid-1940s, he often sent the horns off into the wings and featured an unusual quartet that included his vibraharpist, Milt "Bags" Jackson, and "Diz's rhythm section": John Lewis on piano, Ray Brown on bass, and Kenny "Klook" Clarke on drums. This was the start of the Modern Jazz Quartet.

In the early 1950s, with the Gillespie Orchestra disbanded, Jackson contacted his former colleagues about forming a quartet. They became the Milt Jackson Quartet. This M (Milt) J (Jackson) Q (quartet) was the next step.

In late 1952, when Ray Brown left and bassist Percy Heath came on board, the Jackson four became a cooperative known as the Modern Jazz Quartet. With one personnel change (Connie Kay replaced Klook on drums in 1955), the MJQ would play together for most of the next forty years.

The Modern Jazz Quartet offered the composing genius of John Lewis. His requiem piece for guitarist Django Reinhardt, "Django," is *the* masterpiece of his many classics. Milt Jackson's earthy playing provided contrast with the cooler reflections of pianist Lewis. Bassist Heath and drummer Kay also offered contrast. Most of the time their concept was elegance, but when called upon, they powered the band with fire.

The Quartet's tight playing and understanding of BeBop, Cool Jazz, Hard Bop, Third Stream, and the blues made them one of the most important ensembles in jazz history.

SONNY ROLLINS | 1930–

A number of outstanding teenage saxophonists played in Harlem during the mid-1940s, dreaming of being the next Coleman Hawkins, Charlie Parker, or Lester Young. One of them reached such stature. That Saxophone Colossus is Sonny Rollins.

A music student from childhood, as a professional tenor saxophonist, Theodore Walter Rollins was making classic BeBop sides with Bud Powell and J.J. Johnson by the age of nineteen. Next Rollins began making high-profile sessions with Miles Davis. Soon he made his own dates for Prestige. But for all this early prominence, Rollins's real emergence came a few years later.

Sonny Rollins was dominant in the 1950s styles: Hard Bop, jazz in waltz time, bands with no piano, and extended improvisation. From 1955 to 1957, Rollins's music was part of a package with drummer Max Roach (which also included Clifford Brown until the trumpeter's death in 1956). In November 1957, he struck out on his own. Sonny became the most important new tenor saxophonist in jazz, eventually to share that honor with John Coltrane.

Since the end of the 1960s, Sonny Rollins has been the most esteemed and accomplished of all living jazz tenors, with numerous small groups, many albums, and countless awards. Highlights include the original *Alfie* soundtrack and the everlastingly popular calypso number "St. Thomas."

The trump suit of Sonny Rollins, though, is his moving, well-connected, long-form solos. He is the master, as a listen to "Blue Seven," "The Freedom Suite," "East Broadway Run Down," and "Alfie's Theme" will demonstrate.

SIDNEY BECHET | 1897–1959

On clarinet and soprano saxophone, Sidney Bechet was the most compelling and virtuosic improviser of all the earliest jazz players. His inventions are pivotal to jazz's transition from a folk music centered around a collective ensemble to the art form of individual spontaneous expression.

At age six, the Creole Bechet picked up an older brother's clarinet and soon was sitting in with professionals. Among the first New Orleanians to take jazz north, Bechet was in Chicago when Will Marion Cook heard him and brought him to Europe. There, Sidney was both musically revolutionary and a popular sensation. He even played for the king of England. During this period, Bechet adopted the soprano saxophone, becoming its true pioneer.

Bechet's recordings upon his return to the U.S. were among jazz's first illustrations of improvisation. Bechet joined an early Ellington band, greatly enhancing Duke's jazz knowledge and abilities. He also started a nightclub, an entrepreneurial first for a jazz musician.

Bechet returned to Europe in 1925 and missed the rewards of his trailblazing. Worse, his homecoming coincided with the Great Depression. He briefly left music, but with the Swing Era, Bechet bounced back, dominating the revival of interest in jazz's roots and pioneers. His hit "Summertime" helped launch Blue Note Records and was followed by a prestigious contract with the Victor label.

Sidney Bechet returned to France in 1949 to headline one of the first jazz festivals and decided to stay, becoming one of that country's most celebrated individuals.

THELONIOUS MONK | 1917–1982

Thelonious Sphere Monk, pianist and one of jazz's few genius composers, had an unusual name and a career of remarkable ironies and triumphs.

Monk emerged as a professional pianist shortly after high school. It was the top of the Swing Era, when jazz's fortunes surged. Monk was working and writing many of his classic pieces, but was largely ignored by the press until after his thirtieth birthday.

BeBop had entered the scene, and Monk's compositions were gaining attention. BeBop musicians loved the thoroughly written tunes, but his own highly personalized piano playing and jazz solo concept is distinct from BeBop. During BeBop's and Hard Bop's heyday, Monk's melodies were better known in versions by others than from his own first records for Blue Note and Prestige.

A reversal occurred in 1957 — jazz's illustration of the adage "Life begins at forty." When Monk signed with Riverside Records, they packaged him differently. Monk's first Riverside album was a Duke Ellington songbook, while the second featured chestnuts of American popular song. But the third album's charm was the unleashing of Monk. Thelonious also forged a band, debuting his quartet (featuring John Coltrane) at the legendary Five Spot club. It was the biggest performance success of his career, and although Coltrane moved on, the Thelonious Monk Quartet remained one of the top five working jazz units for more than a decade. In 1964, *Time* magazine put Monk on its cover, the height of his prominence coming ironically during the nadir in jazz's popularity.

EUBIE BLAKE | 1883–1983

Eubie Blake informed us that it wasn't jazz but *ragtime* that we had been listening to all along. The pioneering ragtime pianist made his point by playing great "jazz" from the 1890s to the 1980s. His career alone eclipses in length the lives of Louis Armstrong, John Coltrane, Duke Ellington, Coleman Hawkins, Charlie Parker, and Lester Young.

The parents of James Hubert Blake, born slaves, brought a keyboard instrument into their home and had Eubie taking lessons from the age of six. Blake became one of the East Coast–based ragtime piano players whose impact on early jazz is direct, heard best in the Stride piano of James P. Johnson and Fats Waller.

Eubie Blake was also a composer. His lyricist and partner was vocalist Noble Sissle. They worked for the short-lived James Reese Europe. After Europe's untimely death, it was his associates Sissle & Blake who brought black performers to the Broadway stage with the 1921 hit musical *Shuffle Along*.

The success of that show, plus hit songs such as "I'm Just Wild About Harry" and "Memories of You," made Eubie Blake a star. He led a band for years, wrote more successful songs, settled in Brooklyn, and retired in 1946.

A quarter century later, with jazz music enjoying a mini-revival, the rediscovery of this *pre*-jazz giant led to a second period of pop status for the octogenarian, nonagenarian, and, briefly, centenarian Eubie Blake.

SARAH VAUGHAN | 1924–1990

Sarah Vaughan is BeBop's greatest singer. Sarah sang BeBop so divinely that non-jazz listeners considered it pop, and Vaughan became a star.

As a child, Sarah Lois Vaughan sang in her church's choir, and by age twelve, she was also the organist. Sarah's professional career began at eighteen. Just nineteen, she hit it big under Earl Hines, with whom she sang and played piano. Also in the band were Dizzy Gillespie and Charlie Parker.

Sarah heard and learned their concept quickly. Her genius allowed her to capture the essence of BeBop as a vocalist. On December 31, 1944, she made her first records. With Dizzy on board, she made the first recording of his "A Night in Tunisia," using words that briefly renamed the piece "Interlude." On her second date, she had both Diz *and* Bird. The records sold, and she was on her way.

Sarah recorded hits for Musicraft (1946–1949), Columbia (1949–1954), Mercury (1954–1959), and Roulette (1960–1963). Fewer big sellers came during her last twenty-five years of recording, but one of her final projects was singing the poems of the late Pope John Paul II set to music. Backed by a jazz orchestra in jazz's (and the pope's) answer to rock's *We Are the World,* this album was called *The Planet Is Alive … Let It Live!*

FATS WALLER | 1904–1943

During the Swing Era, Fats Waller was as popular as any jazz figure. Born five years after the Duke, Fats would write as many standards and have even more big hits than Ellington. His singing and sense of humor were the equal of Satchmo's. And nobody played Harlem Stride piano better than he.

Thomas Wright Waller's father was a street preacher, and young Fats, always heavy, accompanied his dad's sermons on a small pump organ. He took piano lessons and was determined to be a musician after hearing Paderwerski at Carnegie Hall in 1915. Waller would grow up to perform there, too, and he got there by playing jazz.

Early on he specialized in a style called Harlem Stride. It sounded a bit like ragtime, but was more rhythmically fluid. Young Fats was also a gifted organist and composer of pop songs, presenting all these gifts on the prestigious Victor label. He was a featured performer on early radio and wrote music for three Broadway shows. Fats played Carnegie Hall for the first time at the age of twenty-three.

Somewhere in the midst of all of this, it was discovered that Waller not only wrote hit songs but that he could sing them as well, and with humor. In 1934, he organized an ensemble called Fats Waller and His Rhythm. It would be a rare small-group success in the big-band years of the Swing Era. Their records on Victor were even more colossal than Waller's 1920s output.

BIX BEIDERBECKE | 1903–1931

Bix Beiderbecke, who played the trumpet-like cornet, was a giant of improvisation who, alongside Louis Armstrong and Sidney Bechet, put the individual artist into the foreground of jazz during the 1920s. His early impact also included the creation of a ballad concept for the new music. Bix's breakthrough allowed jazz to be both sweet and hot at the same time.

A child prodigy, Beiderbecke's musical gifts weren't harnessed until he heard his first jazz records at the age of fifteen. Until then Bix had played piano by ear for occasional amusement; now he focused on training himself to play the cornet—the dominant instrument of New Orleans Jazz.

Bix Beiderbecke soon began playing professionally and became a sensation in the Midwest with the Wolverine Orchestra. Although the Wolverines reflected in concept and repertoire the first New Orleans combos, guided by Bix, they also understood and embraced the emergence of the solo: improvised variants on the theme.

Playing hot jazz solos became Bix's specialty. Important orchestras with limited jazz content hired him to pour on the jazz at specific moments in their programs or on their records. This led to a recording contract with OKeh Records, where he would record the first demonstrations of true jazz ballad playing.

Often returning to his first instrument, the piano, Bix wrote imaginative compositions that combined jazz and western classical, including the famous "In a Mist."

Beiderbecke was short-lived, undoubtedly due to his drinking problem.

LESTER YOUNG | 1909–1959

Lester Young, a tenor saxophonist, was the primary soloist in the original Count Basie Orchestra and Billie Holiday's favorite accompanist. "Prez," as Young was known, helped relax the rhythm of jazz, while creating an entire style for the tenor sax and improvising some of the most inspired and melodic phrases in jazz history.

Young's father was a very early jazz musician who left New Orleans in 1919, taking a band of family members on the road. Little Lester was the drummer, but he switched to saxophone in his mid-teens. As the 1920s progressed, he became the key soloist in the family orchestra and soon moved on. Highlights of his early career include short stretches with King Oliver and Fletcher Henderson.

Kansas City, where he met and befriended the great Count Basie, became the center of Prez's musical world. Young got on board when Basie took a Swing Era big band out of K.C. to great national success.

Young starred in that band from 1936 to 1940, rejoining it from 1943 to 1944. In between, he had tried to lead his own units, but his preference for small groups at the peak of the big-band era limited his potential.

Only after World War II did Young became a star in his own right, touring with the original Jazz at the Philharmonic, Norman Granz's concertized jam sessions. Prez also had hit records throughout the late 1940s.

This pattern—small Young-led combos, records, and JATP touring—remained Young's work regimen for the rest of his life.

DIZZY GILLESPIE | 1917–1993

For Dizzy Gillespie, the trumpet was never enough—he was also compelled to compose and arrange. In addition, Diz explored the world, literally and figuratively, and became the most important musician in jazz's merger with Latino music. Only Satchmo could match Dizzy for bringing jazz to the world.

The teenage John Birks "Dizzy" Gillespie became the hot trumpet specialist in the Teddy Hill Orchestra, a band that played the Savoy Ballroom, toured Europe, broadcast regularly over the NBC network, and recorded for the Victor label. Dizzy next took on the solo trumpet chair in Cab Calloway's big band.

While on tour, Dizzy met Charlie "Bird" Parker and instantly recognized his musical soul mate. Over the next few years, the pair created a new language for jazz called BeBop. Gillespie next formed a big band, which played the new concept but was successful in the Swing Era. His Carnegie Hall debut in 1947 set attendance records. But like most big bands, the Dizzy Gillespie Orchestra went bust in 1950. For several years, Dizzy led small groups and toured with Jazz at the Philharmonic.

In 1956, the U.S. State Department sponsored a new Dizzy Gillespie Orchestra for goodwill touring. When federal funding ended, Dizzy went on to present his big-band music in ensembles assembled just for a given tour, concert, or album. He also led combos, usually adding an unusual instrument to the lineup such as vibes, electric guitar, or flute. In all his endeavors, Diz connected jazz to other forms of Afro-European music forged in the New World. Today, he could and should be seen as a pioneer of World Music.

NOTES ON THE POETIC FORMS

ABSTRACT POEM
Like abstract painters, abstract poets concentrate more on their medium than on what they're actually portraying — but instead of colored paint, their "medium" is sound. The sounds in an abstract poem, can be as small as phonemes, the shortest units of speech (for example, *s* of *sin* versus *ch* of *chin*), or as large as common words and even phrases. Even when they form traditional sentence structures, the words of an abstract poem usually convey sound or feeling instead of meaning. In **Ornette Coleman**, notice how the poet begins with and returns to the tonic, or root, sound in the poem (the letter *O*) as he travels chromatically up the "scale" of the alphabet: *O-A, O-B, O-C, O-D,* and so on. (Also see *Word Play*.)

ACCUMULATIVE POEM
An accumulative poem builds by adding words and phrases into an established rhythm. Sound patterns such as alliteration (repeating a sound or syllable across two or more words) can enhance the effect. **Louis Armstrong** uses alliteration while building from one to twelve words per line, paying homage to the twelve measures of the blues, and can be likened to a long crescendo. In fact, the poem itself is shaped like a dynamic marking on its side — a shape also reminiscent of the letter *A*. (For a related form, see *List Poem*. For more on **Louis Armstrong**, see *Calligram*.)

ACROSTIC
From the Greek words for head or end (*akron*) and line (*stikhos*), as in line of poetry, an acrostic uses the first letter of each line to spell out another word or phrase. In many cultures, creating acrostics — particularly at top speed — has been considered a good exercise for increasing one's mental agility. Did you notice the three acrostics-within-an-acrostic tucked inside **Modern Jazz Quartet**? (For a related form, see *Word Play*. For another acrostic, see **Eubie Blake**.)

ALPHABET POEM
Using the alphabet itself as subject and object, an alphabet poem celebrates the raw letter forms of the English language individually and/or their chemistry together. The alphabet poem can take the shape of a letter of the alphabet (see **Louis Armstrong**); it also can be highly alliterative. It can move through the alphabet by featuring only words that begin with each letter in turn, or it can highlight the sounds of the letters from *A* to *Z* (see **Ornette Coleman**). In a way, the entire book of *Jazz A·B·Z* could be considered a twenty-six-part alphabetic poem — one that also covers the great figures of jazz, from the "alpha" to the "zenith." Its very first word is *Armstrong*, standing in for the letter *A*, and its very last word is *Dizzy*, the *Z* word — with myriad other words in between!

BALLAD
In jazz, a ballad connotes any slow, romantic song. In the narrative poetic tradition, a ballad is specifically a story-song. Ballads tend to focus on a climactic event or ill-fated situation in a character's life, and the storyteller often remains impartial even as catastrophe strikes. Preliterate or illiterate people passed along stories and legends through the singing and recitation of ballads. In **Bix Beiderbecke**, the poet uses the present tense and rhyming, alternating lines of eight and six syllables to involve his readers in the bittersweet life story of this hero of solo jazz improvisation and early master of the jazz ballad.

BEAT POEM
Some say the innovative master of free verse, Walt Whitman, was the original Beat poet. Others see a precedent in the trance writings of William Butler Yeats and his wife, George. But most people associate the Beats with the jazz-loving cluster of "automatic writers" founded by Jack Kerouac, William S. Burroughs, and Allen Ginsberg. From the 1940s through the 1960s, these poets followed their powerful urge for a new form of self-expression that could reveal the "beatific" (hope, ecstasy, spontaneity) inside the "beat" (downtrodden, beat-up, down and out). The poetic homage to **Sidney Bechet** uses methods favored by the Beat Generation — free verse, the list form, alliteration, and a stream-of-consciousness style — in a sibilant ode to the saxophonist's virtuosic, improvisational, spontaneous solo style.

BLUES POEM
A blues song has a basic repeating twelve-bar form, with three sections of four measures each. This pattern is a trellis in its simplicity, allowing for musicians and singers to flower with expression and creativity. The typical blues poem follows this same form, with stanzas of three lines each. These three lines follow a call-and-response pattern called *AAB*. *A* calls attention to a problem or lays out a fact; then *A* is repeated (sometimes with a slight variation). The third line, *B*, responds to and resolves the situation. With his understated piano style and perfect sense of timing, **Count Basie** was the most dramatic of blues pianists. His orchestra personified swinging the blues in the most down-home and elegant of fashions. For anyone who loves to dance, Basie's band is the best.

CALLIGRAM
Derived from the Greek *kalli-* and *gramma*, meaning beautiful letter or piece of writing, and coined by the French writer Guillaume Apollinaire around 1918, a calligram makes the shape of the poem relate to its subject. A close relative of (and sometimes labeled interchangeably with) a concrete poem, a calligram plays with typographic treatment and the literal shaping of lines on the page to turn a poem into a piece of visual artwork. In **Eubie Blake**, the vertical adjectives create ten fingers of meaning like hands on a keyboard, enhanced by the visual rendering underneath. In **Louis Armstrong**, the shape of the poem resembles the letter *A*, which functions in harmony with the alliterative, accumulative nature of the poem and makes a statement that Armstrong is in the *A* position on the roster of jazz history. On the cover of this book, the title, subtitle, and bylines project from the author's horn like musical sound waves — another calligram.

FREE VERSE
Free verse doesn't depend on rhyme, nor on a regular meter of stressed and unstressed syllables — it's "free" of most rules. What makes it verse rather than rhythmic prose is its heightened, condensed language and a repeating pattern of cadences, phrases, or images. These patterns can be visual as well as aural. Easing the rules of meter gives the poet a wider choice of vocabulary and results in a natural, modern sound. **Charles Mingus**'s highly original and supremely diverse world of music will also be forever natural and modern.

HAIKU
Haiku has been called a "dance on the blade" — it is intended to make the reader perceive the essence of a moment of experience. A haiku should be brief. The reader fills in the empty spaces using his or her own emotions and imagination. It usually invokes the physical senses and often mentions time or season. Its form is three short fragments, all in the present tense, with the middle one a bit longer than the other two and no rhyme. Many writers of haiku in English adhere to a strict syllabic count (often 5-7-5), but this is not necessarily an accurate translation of the intentions behind the traditional Japanese form. What a good haiku must do is create a sharp, pure, and resonant image, like the deep-song sound of **Thelonious Monk**'s piano and the short, distinctive themes that characterize his compositions.

INSULT POEM

King Oliver was full of humor. He could make his horn sound exactly like a baby crying or a woman laughing. And he also loved to "play the dozens." Here's one crack he made: "Son, you have a head on you. So has a mug of beer."

Still don't know what an insult poem is? Catch the *K* page for what King says to the college kid. Or better yet, take this tip for the next time you're with some wise mouths yourself. When somebody says something clever about you, make yourself laugh, even while your face is turning hot. Guess what? You've been insulted by a *poet*. Just remember the old saying: "Sticks and stones . . ." Or better yet, send your own "poem" back by reply.

LIMERICK

With its rhyme scheme *AABBA*, the five-line limerick has been identified as the only form of English-language poetry used solely for humor. The first, second, and fifth lines have three stressed syllables, or beats, and the third and fourth lines only two. Usually the rhythm is anapestic, two unstressed syllables followed by a stressed one. Sometimes the last line of the poem is a variant of the first; often it contains a clever twist. In **Gerry Mulligan**, three stanzas in limerick form with a stand-alone coda pay tribute to the first gentleman of Cool, his music, and the "Mulligan mood" created in his listeners and fans. (For More on *meter*, see *Meter Play*.)

LIST POEM

Now often written purely for enjoyment, the list poem is a simple but ancient form. At one time, it was even functional — it was a way to remember things. List poems feature very personal and specific imagery, and they often follow the shape of an arc, like a well-crafted story. The use of consistent stylistic devices gives them cohesion. The list poem **John Coltrane** tells the story of the great saxophonist while developing like one of his own complicated improvisations — a central theme spins out many related ideas, then another central theme follows with its development, and so on.

LYRIC POEM

One of the three major types of poetry (the other two are dramatic and narrative), a lyric poem is most like a piece of music in its meter, rhyme, and cadence. Not as structured as some poetic forms, its main purpose usually is to express a sensual, subjective emotion felt by the poet. In ancient Greece, poets often sang or recited poetry accompanied by a stringed instrument called the lyre. Lyric poems written today still give the feeling that they could be sung; they are intimate, personal, and can reveal the poet's own sense of mortality — just like a recording by **Lady Day**.

METER PLAY

A poem featuring meter play is challenging for the poet and rewarding for the listener. Best when read aloud, meter play showcases a variety of rhythms and is an ideal form for a poem about music.

Like a composition with changing time signatures, the five stanzas of **Duke Ellington** explore five different rhythmic patterns. The first stanza features dactyls, metric feet of three syllables each. The first syllable is accented, as the first beat of a triplet might be in a musical composition (DUM-dah-dah).

The second stanza also features three-syllable feet, but here the accent is on the last syllable in each foot (dah-dah-DUM), which is called an anapest.

The third stanza plays with eight syllables and the equally weighted foot (DUM-DUM) called a spondee. With its punchy, consonant-heavy words, this stanza has a staccato beat.

The fourth stanza experiments with iambs (dah-DUM), stressing the second and usually fourth syllables, with ten beats per line.

With longer, flowing lines, the last stanza inverts the iambic rhythm to close the poem with an extended meditation in the shuffle rhythm, the root rhythm of swing (SHUH-fle, SHUH-fle). Ancient Greek poets might call this shuffle foot a trochee, after the verb *trekhein* (to run) — but would they swing it?

NURSERY RHYME

"Oh, there's none so rare as can compare / with King Cole and his fiddlers three." Nursery rhymes are poems or songs for children that are passed down orally, sometimes for centuries, and their origins often are lost. No one can be sure which historical figure was behind the nursery rhyme legend of Old King Cole. Some say it was a Celtic king from 300 C.E.; others say that because of the vocabulary, the rhyme couldn't have been written before 1585. However, the Gaelic word for music is *ceol* (pronounced "kole"), which is perhaps prophecy. **Nat "King" Cole** was ready early for a life of music — he made his first public performance at the age of four.

ODE

What makes an ode an ode has changed quite a lot over the past 2,500 years. Classical odes were highly complex in their meter and stanza structure, featuring repetition, formal language, an exalted tone, and heightened poetic devices. Modern poets have rediscovered the traditional form but also use odes to pay homage to personal and everyday topics. The word *ode* comes from the Greek word *aeidein*, which means to sing or to chant, and most odes feature the same kind of emotional intensity that a singer or musician brings to her work. **Jelly Roll Morton** loved to talk about himself — that's why an ode is the perfect form for his biography. This particular example of the form celebrates its subject with patterned incantations. Its unique use of the vernacular, its compelling imagery, and its underlying message show that the musician and his contributions will stand the test of time — just like the ode.

PANTOUM

Originally a fifteenth-century Malayan poetic form, in English the pantoum now means a poem in which the second and fourth lines of each stanza reappear as the first and third lines of the next one. This pattern can continue on through a poem of any length. The final stanza often features the third line of the first stanza as its second line and the first line of the poem as the last line, and thus each line is used twice. In **Charlie Parker**, the poet follows this challenging form as a way of paying tribute to Bird's complex musical style while also making use of the improvisational properties of substitution. (See *Substitution Poem*.)

PERFORMANCE POEM

Poetry recited to music is the essence of ritual, and the reenactment of events through ritual is the essence of all the performing arts. In ancient times and modern, with roots deep into many African and other cultures, performance poems have often taken place to the rhythm of a drumbeat. **Abdullah Ibn Buhaina** features an interwoven score of spoken words and finger-snapped beats that pays tribute to legendary drummer and bandleader Art Blakey.

PREACHED POEM

The dialogue between the preacher and the congregation follows one of the oldest communication patterns in human history—call and response. Deeply imbedded in African American tradition, having been brought to America by West African slaves, it is used in civic and religious settings as a ritual that encourages group participation. The speaker's "call" is punctuated by the group's "response." The dialogue can be both spontaneous and rhythmic, like the inspired interplay of a soloist backed by a chorus. Call and response is also a common element of many musical forms, from the classical sonata to rhythm and blues. Just as a charismatic preacher depends upon his voice, **Ella Fitzgerald** used her incomparable vocal instrument to evoke deep emotional responses and a devoted, reverential following among her listeners.

PROSE POEM

A prose poem is similar to a lyric poem but is written on the page like a passage of prose. It doesn't have line breaks or rhyme, but it tends to be short. As with lyric poetry, the poet's intention is usually to clearly create an emotional impact—a prose poem should read with a freshness of language and a sense of rhythm, and the imagery should be dense enough to give the reader a feeling of intensity. In **Fats Waller**, one dynamic evening in the presence of the great pianist is contained within the flexible walls of this form.

RONDEAU

A rondeau is a poem of thirteen lines, divided into stanzas of five, three, and five lines, plus a refrain that repeats at the end of the second and the third stanza for a total of fifteen lines. The refrain is also the first line of the poem. Traditionally, the rhyme scheme is fairly important, but near rhyme (matching consonants without matching vowels) can substitute for true end rhyme. The French word *rond*, meaning round, is the root of the rondeau—and the repeating refrains give the poem the circular feeling of a round that is sung. In **Sonny Rollins**, even the last name of the subject of the poem "radiates roundness."

SKELTONIC VERSE

Invented by English poet John Skelton (ca. 1460–1529) and favored by rap and hip-hop artists today, skeltonic verse, or tumbling verse, features short lines of few syllables whose end rhymes continue as long as the poet can keep it up—and when one end rhyme ends, another begins. Slant rhyme (also called near rhyme) is acceptable, as is rejet, where one part of a grammatical phrase rolls over to the next line. Skeltonic verse has power, punch, and humor—all appropriate choices for the peripatetic, pioneering **Dizzy Gillespie**. (For a definition of *near rhyme*, see *Rondeau*.)

SONNET

In Italian, *sonetto*; in Old Provençal, *sonet*, a little sound or song: a sonnet. Fourteen carefully crafted lines around a single idea, the sonnet is traditionally written in iambic pentameter (five iambs per line) and very often has to do with love. Whether or not line spaces are used, the organization of a sonnet is often broken into an octet (eight lines), a quartet (four lines), and a concluding couplet (two lines). In **Sarah Vaughan**, the emotional climax at the end of the eighth line leads to the traditional *volta*, or new turn of thought, in the next four lines. In a unique approach, the final couplet departs from the first-person singular to a plural voice, creating the feeling of an orchestra rejoining a singer for the finale—although the whole sonnet remains unified in its declaration of devotion to the diva. (For a definition of *iamb*, see *Meter Play*.)

SUBSTITUTION POEM

In this substitution poem about **Coleman Hawkins**, a fairly straightforward prose statement is reiterated piece by piece through an extended improvisation of words that convey, ultimately, the same meaning as the original. The concept of substitution features prominently in all kinds of poetic imagery, where a word or description metaphorically stands in, or "substitutes," for another physical experience or an idea—still leaving a clear image or impression in the mind of the reader. The process of substitution, whether reharmonizing or reprising with variations, is also important in music and especially in jazz.

TANKA

Tanka is an ancient form of Japanese court poetry, even older than haiku, dating back at least 1,300 years and traditionally presented as the finale at most special occasions. In written Japanese, the poem might appear as one line, but in English, traditionally a poem of thirty-one syllables is divided into five lines. As with a haiku, counting syllables is unimportant if the five-line form (short-long-short-long-long) produces a unified poem true to the original tanka spirit, which in content can be quite flexible. **Lester Young**, nearly the finale of *Jazz A•B•Z*, uses the form to create an image of tonal and visual color that evokes the intensity this melodic tenor saxophonist could command at even the softest volumes.

WORD PLAY

Witty, original, rhythmic, dancing—word play creates a sensory experience for both writer and reader. Patterns lightly applied yield meanings that are both intentional and unexpected; sounds that are juxtaposed, layered, and contrasting please and provoke the ear ("ditto" the music of **Miles Davis**). Elements the poet can play with include acrostics, alliteration, assonance (echoing vowel sounds across words when consonants differ), and consonance (consonants repeated across words whose main vowel sounds differ). In this poem, words of five letters each line up in two columns under the starting consonants of *M* and *D* to tout the legacy of the pioneering and prophetic trumpeter. (For a definition of *alliteration*, see *Accumulative Poem*. For related forms, see *Meter Play* and *Abstract Poem*.)

Wynton Marsalis has been described as the most outstanding jazz artist and composer of his generation. He has helped propel jazz to the forefront of American culture through his brilliant performances, recordings, broadcasts, and compositions as well as through his leadership as the artistic director of Jazz at Lincoln Center (JALC). Mr. Marsalis is the music director of the world-renowned Lincoln Center Jazz Orchestra, which spends more than half the year on tour. He also hosts the popular Jazz for Young People concerts and helped lead the effort to construct JALC's new home, Frederick P. Rose Hall, the first education, performance, and broadcast facility devoted to jazz, which opened in October 2004.

Mr. Marsalis was born in New Orleans in 1961. He began his classical training on the trumpet at age twelve and entered the Juilliard School at age seventeen. That same year, he joined Art Blakey and the Jazz Messengers, the acclaimed band in which generations of emerging jazz artists honed their craft, and subsequently made his recording debut as a leader in 1982. Since then, he has made more than forty jazz and classical recordings, earning nine Grammy Awards. In 1983, he became the first and only artist to win classical and jazz Grammys in the same year and repeated this feat in 1984. His rich body of compositions includes the oratorio *Blood on the Fields*, for which he was awarded the first-ever Pulitzer Prize in music for a jazz composition.

Mr. Marsalis is an internationally respected teacher and spokesperson for music education and has received honorary doctorates from dozens of universities and colleges throughout the United States. Britain's senior conservatoire, the Royal Academy of Music, granted Mr. Marsalis honorary membership, the Academy's highest decoration for a non-British citizen. In France, the Ministry of Culture awarded him the most prestigious decoration of the French Republic, the rank of Knight in the Order of Arts and Literature. He also was appointed as a U.N. Messenger of Peace by the Secretary-General of the United Nations in 2001.

A resident of New York City, Mr. Marsalis is the father of three boys, ages seventeen, fifteen, and nine.

ABOUT PAUL ROGERS

Paul Rogers has more than twenty-five years of experience as an illustrator and poster artist. His clients include the National Academy of Recording Arts and Sciences, Pixar Pictures, the Playboy Jazz Festival, the Seattle International Film Festival, the Southern Poverty Law Center, and Warner Bros. Studios. He created the official poster for the New Orleans Jazz and Heritage Festival in 2002 and 2004, and also for Super Bowl XXXVII. His work has won awards from the American Institute of Graphic Arts, the Association of Illustrators/London, the Society of Illustrators/New York, *American Illustration*, *Communication Arts*, *Graphis Poster*, and *Print*. His drawings and paintings have been exhibited at the Stella Jones Gallery in New Orleans and at the Mendenhall Sobieski Gallery in Pasadena, California. He is a graduate of the Art Center College of Design, and is now a member of the faculty. Rogers spends most of his time in his studio — where the music is always on. He lives in Pasadena with his wife, graphic designer Jill von Hartmann; his children, Alexandra and Nate; and their two cats, Louis Armstrong and Harry "Sweets" Edison.

ABOUT PHIL SCHAAP

Jazz historian Phil Schaap serves as curator of Jazz at Lincoln Center. As an educator, he has taught jazz at the graduate level at Columbia University and Rutgers University, and he continues his academic teaching career at Princeton University. Schaap has been broadcasting jazz on the radio for thirty-five years on WKCR and has won Grammy Awards for historical writing, producing, and audio engineering.

ACKNOWLEDGMENTS

My thanks to Frank Stewart, Raymond "Big Boss" Murphy, Mademoiselle John, and Baby Rat Mousse Pie

—W. M.

I would like to thank the photographers whose irreplaceable work inspired some of the portraits in this book: Joe Alper, Bruehl-Bourges, William Claxton, William Gottlieb, Norman Granz, Don Hunstein, Herman Leonard, Bob Parent, Jan Persson, and Lee Tanner. I would also like to acknowledge the work of the artists and designers who have been major influences on this project: Paul Colin, Stuart Davis, Miguel Covarrubias, Jim Flora, Al Hirschfeld, David Stone Martin, Pierre Merlin, Paul Rand, Cliff Roberts, and most of all, Alex Steinweiss.

I'm grateful to Phil Schaap for his erudite contribution to this book and his generous willingness to share. I am continuously amazed by his knowledge of jazz music and history.

I want to thank Karen Lotz and Chris Paul at Candlewick Press for their support and belief in this book throughout the creative process.

A special note of thanks to my agent, Sally Heflin, who saw the project very early on and did so much to make it become a reality.

And thank you to Blue Trimarchi at Art Works for his valuable expertise and even more, his friendship.

It is impossible for me to overstate the importance of Jill von Hartmann to the design of this book, and to my life.

—P. R.